D0855688

A THEORY OF PARTIES AND ELECTORAL SYSTEMS

Richard S. Katz teaches political science
at The Johns Hopkins University

RICHARD S. KATZ

A Theory of Parties and Electoral Systems

The Johns Hopkins University Press / Baltimore and London

The Johns Hopkins University Press, Baltimore, Maryland 21218
The Johns Hopkins Press Ltd., London

Library of Congress Cataloging in Publication Data
Katz, Richard S.
   A theory of parties and electoral systems.
   Includes bibliographical references and index.
   1. Political parties. 2. Elections. I. Title.
JF2051.K33   324   80–8019
ISBN 0–8018–2435–4

For Judith

Contents

Preface   xi

1. Parties, Elections, and Democracy   1

2. Electoral Law   17

3. An Extensive Test   35

4. An Intensive Test: Electoral Experience   60

5. An Intensive Test: Campaign and Nomination   84

6. An Intensive Test: Verification   100

7. Concluding Remarks   115

   Appendix A. Sampling   125

   Appendix B. Questionnaire   127

   Notes   133

   Index   147

Figures

2.1. Placement of seven parties in a hypothetical two-dimensional
issue space   23
2.2. Territories of five parties in a two-dimensional issue space
with demonstration that each must appeal to voters with
diametrically opposing interests   25
2.3. Placement of four parties in a hypothetical two-dimensional
issue space with the political territory of party *B* mapped
under PR   27
2.4. Placement of four parties in a hypothetical two-dimensional
issue space with the political territory of party *B* mapped in
pairwise competition with each other party under plurality
election   27
4.1. Graphic representation of relationship between electoral
system and ideological politics   68

Tables

3.1. Parties and electoral system characteristics   38
3.2. Ideology as indicated by issue extremism on individual
issues versus electoral formula   44
3.3. Ideology as indicated by number of extreme issue positions
taken, policy consistency, and doctrinism versus electoral
formula   46
3.4. Issue orientation as indicated by number of low clarity
issue positions versus district magnitude   50
3.5. Issue orientation as indicated by issue and ideological
debate versus district magnitude   51
3.6. Issue orientation as indicated by the importance of purposive
incentives versus district magnitude   52
3.7. Issue orientation as indicated by number of low clarity
positions versus nature of choice   54
3.8. Issue orientation as indicated by issue and ideological debate
and the importance of purposive incentives versus nature of choice 55
3.9. Factionalism versus preference voting   56
3.10. Number of party leaders versus preference voting   58
4.1. Frequency distributions of number of significant parties
per constituency   69
4.2. Number of competitive constellations (N) by year   70
4.3. Mean absolute deviation between parties' shares of seats and
votes (proportionality) by year   71
4.4. Interelection changes (in percentages) in votes (dV) and
seats (dS)   72
4.5. Interelection gains and losses of seats   73
4.6. Percentage variance in vote shares explained by national factors 74

4.7. Interelection turnover of incumbents 75
4.8. Italian electoral result by list position, 1972 76
4.9. Frequency distribution of Kendall's tau between list order
and electoral order for middle section of DC lists, 1972 77
4.10. Preference votes cast in Italy as a percentage of total possible, 1968 78
4.11. Reasons for candidate choice given by Italians casting
preference votes in 1958 79
4.12. Reasons for candidate choice given by candidates and party
officials in Italy 80
4.13. Frequency distribution of number of candidates and elected
deputies per constituency, Ireland, 1973 80
4.14. Transfers of votes, Ireland, 1969 and 1973 81
4.15. Reasons for candidate choice given by candidates and party
officials in Ireland 82
5.1. Importance of national and local issues and leaders in
determining constituency electoral results 86
5.2. Candidates stressing national or local issues in campaigning 87
5.3. Candidates stressing various issues in their campaigns 88
5.4. Campaign techniques rated "Important" or "Very Important"
by respondents 89
5.5. Candidates' personal campaign costs 92
5.6. Respondents reporting at least one and two or more national
leaders campaigning in their constituencies 93
5.7. Residence of candidates 97
5.8. Factors ranked as most important in selection of candidates 98
6.1. Deputies' responses to the question, "What is the single most
important part of a deputy's job?" 108

Preface

POLITICAL parties and elections go hand in hand in modern democracies. Modern mass parties were created to contest elections and electoral systems exist to structure competition among parties. Parties and elections are inexorably linked, yet we know very little of the relationship between them. This book represents an attempt partially to fill this gap in understanding. Its aim is to explain party characteristics (the dependent variables) from the nature of the electoral environment in which the party competes (the independent variables).

Any explanation, whether in the guise of a social science theory or based simply on the everyday use of the word *because,* requires a prior set of assumptions about the nature of causation. The theory developed in the following pages is predicated on the assumption that behavior can be understood best as being the result of choices by individuals seeking to attain their goals. It is, thus, based on the rationalistic or economic approach, and an additional aim of the book is to demonstrate the power and usefulness of this approach.

Causation never can be proven outside an experimental setting, if indeed it can be proven there. As a result, the most one can do is to gather evidence that supports the plausibility of one's assertions about causality. For this theory, I have tried to do this in two ways, first by showing that the theory's general conclusions significantly increase our predictive power when applied to data from a large number of countries, and second by showing that the intermediate processes by which those conclusions were reached are approximated well in more detailed data from three countries. In performing these disparate tasks, in developing the original theory, and in transforming it from its beginnings as a dissertation into its present form, I have accumulated a great number of debts, on both sides of the Atlantic. It is a pleasure to be able to acknowledge them here.

In Europe, I am first and most deeply grateful to the politicians who took the time to respond to my questions and to the librarians and government statisticians in London, Dublin, and Rome who helped me assemble the electoral data analyzed. Without them, there could have been no intensive test of the theory. Among professional colleagues, the staff of the Government Department at the University of Essex provided the facilities that made the British and Irish phases of the research possible. In Dublin, Basil Chubb, Brian Farrell, Tom Garvin, and Maurice Manning were more than generous with their insights into Irish politics. In Rome, the staff of COSPOS, and especially Franco Cazzola, gave aid and comfort in a variety of ways.

On this side of the ocean, there are other debts. Funds for the collection of the data used in the intensive test came from a dissertation research grant of the Foreign Area Fellowship Program. Joseph LaPalombara, who was my dissertation advisor and indeed who converted me to the comparative study of politics, was kind enough to read and comment on the entire book manuscript, as were David Mayhew, Sidney Tarrow, and Kenneth Janda. The last was also generous enough to give me prepublication access to the data on which the extensive test of the theory was based. The suggestions of these scholars have greatly increased the clarity of what I have said as well as improving its substance. The readability of the text also has been enhanced greatly by the efforts of Henry Tom and Judie Zubin of The Johns Hopkins University Press. Where errors remain, whether grammatical, factual, or interpretive, it has been my stubbornness and not their lack of effort that has been responsible.

Finally, without my wife, Judith, who did at least some of everything for which I have thanked anyone else, as well as interminable typing, coding, cooking, cleaning, and moving, I can only say that there would have been no book. For her patience and love I am most truly thankful, and to her this book quite deservedly is dedicated.

A THEORY OF PARTIES AND
ELECTORAL SYSTEMS

1

Parties, Elections, and Democracy

$\langle$ MODERN democracy is party democracy; the political institutions and practices that are the essence of democratic government in the Western view were the creations of political parties and would be unthinkable without them.[1] If asked to define Western democracy, one could do little better than to say that it is the selection of major political decision makers through free elections among candidates of competing political parties.[2] Every country that generally would be considered democratic is governed in this way; no country ordinarily called undemocratic is.$\rangle$ Once the scale of society makes direct popular rule impossible and the complexity of political life renders selection by lot unacceptable, representation based on popular election appears the only way to preserve the elements of popular participation, direction, and control implicit in democracy.

Of course, a nation's claim to be called democratic rests as much on the freedom of its elections as on the existence of parties. Competition among candidates of a single party, as in Yugoslavia, does not satisfy Western standards of democracy when others effectively are barred from the contest. Nor does multiparty competition satisfy Western democratic standards when, as in Poland, one party is in fact guaranteed permanent governmental control regardless of popular wishes. While freedom to organize and freedom to compete are defining characteristics of free elections, we still would look askance at nonparty elections in any but the smallest societies. Without parties to structure the campaign, to provide continuity from one election to the next, and to provide links among candidates in different localities and for different offices, the resulting elections are unlikely to be meaningful, even if they are technically free.[3] $\rangle$

Not only does the existence of competing political parties divide the democratic from the nondemocratic. The character of the parties in a political system is intimately related to the quality of its democracy—to the

1

structure and functioning of its political institutions, to the nature of the interests represented or unrepresented and to the distribution of influence among them, to the capacity of the system to solve the society's problems, and indeed to the likely longevity of the democratic regime itself. The nature of the party system is among the explanations given most frequently for the virtues or defects of regimes.

Why has British government, at least until recently, been so effective? Perhaps it is because the British have had two cohesive and policy-oriented parties, each making concrete and specific proposals to the electorate, each able to take effective control of the government if victorious in a general election, and each driven by the desire for electoral victory, and the possibility of such victory, to take moderate and responsible positions, both when in power and out. Thus, the failure of communism in Britain might be traced to the decision of the Conservative party under Disraeli to appeal to the working class rather than to attempt to exclude it from participation as did many conservative parties on the European continent.[4] Why has the Italian government been unable to deal effectively with that country's pressing economic and social problems? Some would argue that it is because the party system of polarized pluralism or imperfect bipartitism encourages irresponsibility on the extremes and inaction in the center.[5] Why did the Weimar Republic collapse? Perhaps interparty bickering prevented a united front by the moderates against the Nazis.[6] Why, indeed, is politics in the West so different from politics in the Soviet bloc, notwithstanding important institutional similarities? One reason is that politics in one system is dominated by a single monolithic party, while in the other, interparty competition is the rule.

Implicit in such accounts of the effects of party systems and structures is a prescription for political parties. If party systems have effects that are good or bad, then it must be possible to evaluate particular systems on the basis of those effects. Ultimately it should be possible to describe the system that would be judged "best" by virtue of minimizing the bad effects and maximizing the good. The most widely accepted candidate for the role of ideal party system is the "responsible two-party government model." This model came to prominence in the United States in the last quarter of the nineteenth century based on admiration for, and misreading of, British practice at that time, but the model fits the actualities of British practice in the third quarter of the twentieth century fairly well.[7] In fact, there have been important differences in both theory and practice between the Labour and Conservative parties, as well as among the American supporters of responsible two-party government, over such questions as internal party democracy and the role of the party leader. As a result, it is more proper to speak of these models in the plural. They all share, however, three basic conclusions that allow them to be considered together here.

These theories all hold that there should be two parties, that they should be cohesive, and that they should be policy oriented. There should be two parties because responsibility means that the people must be able to call some known individuals to account. In coalitions, lines of responsibility are blurred, as each party attempts to blame its partners for failures while taking credit itself for successes. Only when one party is given total control, can that party ultimately be held totally responsible. The existence of only two parties guarantees that one or the other will achieve a majority in any election.

Likewise, the parties should be cohesive because otherwise they may prove incapable of translating their mandates into effective action, and indeed because without cohesion the very concept of an electoral mandate is ambiguous. Only if the party acts together as a team can the voters reward or punish it at the polls as a team. Without cohesion, voters have no way to tell precisely who is to be punished if disaster strikes. Only if each candidate advocates the same policies and can be trusted to act with his copartisans to carry them out are voters in all districts presented with the same choice, yet unless this condition is met, an election cannot truly be said to have given anyone a mandate at all. (In the interests of clarity and parsimony, references to politicians will use masculine pronouns while references to voters will use feminine pronouns. Obviously, this is not to imply that all politicians are male or that all voters are female.) The preference for a two-party system also relates to this point. When there are more than two parties, often there will be many different coalitions capable of producing a majority. Since coalition strategy is not decided by the election but rather by the parties after the election results are known, voters cannot really know the likely impact of their ballots when they cast them.[8] This uncertainty undermines the direct link between voters' preferences and the selection of government officials, obscuring any legitimate claim to an electoral mandate. Finally, since the objective of democracy is to give the people control over public policy, not simply over the allotment of public honors, competition between parties, and agreement within each party, should be based on a shared view of the direction that policy should take.

These conclusions are based on a number of underlying assumptions, about which one may differ, with regard to both the nature of democracy and the nature of society. The responsible parties theorists assume that majority control of policy is the objective to be maximized; it is for this reason that cohesion, bipartitism, and policy orientation are required. American pluralists, however, more concerned with keeping government in check and restraining the power of the majority, have argued for diversity within each party as a brake against extremism.[9] If there are deep cleavages and more than two distinct and important complexes of policy preferences in society, it is hard to see how two parties can be adequately representative if they are also cohesive. In this case either a multiparty system or less cohesive parties might be supported.[10] Where social cleavages are intense, it may be more important to have representation based on racial or ethnic criteria than on policy preferences.[11] Regardless of this disagreement about the answers, there is substantial agreement among political thinkers as to the important questions about any party system. First, how many parties are there: two, a few, or many? Second, on what basis are the parties structured and on what basis do they compete with one another? Are they oriented toward policy questions; patronage; communal, religious, or ethnic groups; or what? Third, what are the parties like internally? Are they dominated by an extragovernmental membership organization or directorate, or are the crucial decisions made by the party's elected office holders? Are the parties internally cohesive, so that the overwhelmingly important political distinction is between parties; or are there distinctions of equal or greater importance within each party? In the latter case, what is the basis of these conflicts, and what form do they take?

In fact, a political party has many functions, some of them obvious and many others more subtle, and correspondingly numerous structural manifestations. For example, parties are organizations of holders of, and aspirants to, elective office. This statement is chosen advisedly, for difficulty might arise with parties of the extreme left or extreme right if the more restrictive definition of parties as organizations that attempt to seize control of the government by actually taking over the principal positions of authority were adopted. Extreme parties often recognize that they have no chance of inclusion in government, and reflect that realization in their actions. Yet surely the characteristic that distinguishes political parties from the many other organizations that attempt to influence policy is the prominence, if not the primacy, given by parties to electoral activity. A related manifestation of party is as an organization of those candidates who were successful electorally, that is, the party in power. This was certainly the origin of modern parties, and it is toward increasing the size of this organization and retaining membership in it that much political activity is directed. Parties also exist as agencies for the propagation of distinctive political viewpoints or ideologies. While one aim of such political education may be electoral victory, numerous examples may be advanced of circumstances in which ideological activists were prepared to sacrifice possible victory to doctrinal purity. Parties frequently serve as the bases of social or cultural activities generally divorced from electoral politics. Other faces of parties could be suggested as well. All this makes party extremely difficult to define in a universally acceptable way.[12] This need not foreclose theorizing about parties, but it points to the necessity of making clear at the outset the aspect or aspects of party to which a particular theory or hypothesis is to apply.

The theory to be suggested in this book applies particularly to legislative parties. This choice was made for two reasons. First, especially in parliamentary systems, but to a great extent in all systems, the legislative party is the most important manifestation of party politics. It represents the collective voice of the party in government, and therefore has the most direct and immediate impact on policy formation. Frequently, the legislative party is the group formally empowered to make party policy, and even when control is vested formally in an extraparliamentary body it is normally the leaders of the legislative party who are also the high officials of the extraparliamentary organization. The party's aim in national electoral politics is to increase the size of its parliamentary delegation. Second, there is reason to believe that it will be easier to theorize about parliamentary parties. There is much truth in the aphorism that two deputies, one of whom is a Revolutionary, have more in common than two revolutionaries, one of whom is a deputy. In particular, the fact that they are composed of full-time or nearly full-time, professional politicians, all of whom depend on reelection for their continued employment, may be expected to impose an element of commonality on all legislative parties. If electoral activity distinguishes political parties from other groups in society, then the fact of election distinguishes parliamentarians from most other party officials.

In focusing on parliamentary parties, many of the questions concerning party systems alluded to above will be explored in a search for the causes of differences among parties. Limited attention will be devoted to the question of party number. Why does a particular system have two parties, as in the United States; a few parties, as in Australia, Germany, and Scandinavia; or many parties, as in Finland and Italy?

More central to the analysis, what explains the difference in the degree to which parliamentary parties are oriented toward policy questions? Most votes taken in legislative bodies are related to public policy, and in this respect all parliamentary parties are obliged to take policy positions. These policy positions may appear to be the basis of legislative party cohesion, as in Britain (at least until recently), or they may cut across party lines, as in the United States. Even when parties vote cohesively, however, there may be no real difference between their policy views or consistency among them. Asked, for example, to place Irish parties on a left-right continuum, one would be hard-pressed to begin. Likewise, the viewpoints embraced within the Italian Christian Democratic party or the Japanese Liberal Democratic party are so widely divergent as to suggest that each party is held together by something other than policy considerations.

How is one to explain differences among parties with respect to cohesion, both the level of cohesion and the form taken by deviations from cohesion? In any large group there will be disagreements. Likewise, so long as the number of choices on each issue is substantially less than the number of members in the group, some members must agree among themselves more often than they agree with others. This observation applies to parliamentary parties as much as to any group. It is not inevitable that these disagreements undermine party cohesion. If intraparty conflict is contained within the party, and if the losers agree to accept the party's decision as binding upon them until changed, the party may still present a united front to the electorate and act cohesively within the legislature. Certainly until recently, and even now to a greater extent than in most countries, British parties exemplified this. The Conservatives have experienced major disagreements between right-wing elements like the Monday Club and the more moderate center, and the Labour party has seen the left frequently dissatisfied with the policies of its less radical leadership. Yet in both cases, the public and politicians could rest assured that once a decision had been made all members would support it with their votes on divisions and in their election campaigns.

When a party fails to act cohesively, it may do so in one of two ways. On the one hand, it may be factionalized. While differences of view will arise in any party, in some parties these disagreements are highly institutionalized. When groups form within parties, groups with leaders able to make decisions that will be honored by a stable following even in cases of individual disagreement and with organizations that penetrate across local boundaries and are independent of the regular party organization, groups that are prepared to act contrary to overall party decisions, then cohesion clearly has broken down. Indeed, under these circumstances, the balance of power within a party may become as important, or more so, than the balance of power between parties. This definition of faction, requiring durability, leadership, and cohesion, is stronger than that often employed.[13] Since some conflict and unity of action among agreeing members must be expected in any party, it seems most useful to reserve the term *faction* for this more advanced form of internal cleavage, in which groups become, in effect, parties within the party. Italian or Japanese parties provide good examples of factionalism.[14]

On the other hand, internal disagreement may result in an amorphous party, with each member operating very much on his or her own. In a sense, this is simply the case in which factionalism has advanced so far that every individual is a faction of one. The extreme multiplication of autonomous actors fundamentally changes the situation, however. While factional leaders may be able to negotiate reasonably stable arrangements allowing the party to act together under most circumstances, when each member is an independent entrepreneur, even *pro forma* unity is unlikely. The sheer number of agreements required to produce unanimity is, of course, increased. Further, while "side payments" in the form of government office may be offered to factional leaders in return for support,[15] there simply are not enough such positions for all members of the parliamentary party. In this case, it is even more clear that there can be no leader capable of assuming responsibility for the actions of the party as a whole. Parties in the American Congress fit this category.

While these examples illustrate a few of the more extreme types of parliamentary parties, in detail the variety of legislative party systems seems limited only by the number of legislatures in which they might be found. Given their importance to the character of democratic government, it is not surprising that countless attempts have been made to explain the structure and functioning of these parties. While a full-scale analysis of previous theories and hypotheses is beyond the scope of this chapter, a brief review of some of the theories advanced to explain just one aspect of parliamentary party systems will provide a useful background for the theory to be advanced in succeeding chapters. For the sake of brevity, attention will be focused only on the problem of party cohesion, and only for the countries cited above as examples.

One common explanation of the cohesion of British parties is the power of the national party leadership over nominations.

Some observers believe that the process of selecting parliamentary candidates . . . plays a leading role in sustaining the cohesion of the parliamentary parties. They point to the fact that the national agencies of both the Conservative and Labour parties . . . enjoy the power to veto any candidate selected by a constituency organization. Such a veto deprives a candidate of the official party label, without which his chances of being elected are slim.[16]

It also has been suggested that the national party leadership can reward loyalty by placing a candidate in a safe constituency. The natural conclusion is that parliamentarians interested in retaining their seats in the House of Commons will heed their leaders' instructions. As Ranney has shown, the national parties have virtually no ability to assign candidates to constituencies, nor have they in ordinary circumstances an effective veto power; a schism is far more costly to the national party than to a constituency organization. Nonetheless, loyalty may be enforced by constituency selection committees, themselves in general "more Tory (or Socialist) than the Leader."[17]

Beyond this, cohesion in British parties has been attributed to the virtual monopolies leaders of the two parties hold over the power of promotion to the front benches. While there are prominent members of the party who must be included in any cabinet, regardless of the leader's wishes, the opportunity to become prominent is very much in the leader's hands. Few backbenchers are likely to be so important that they must be given junior ministries. Still, although "one way [of getting into the Cabinet] is to crawl up the staircase of preferment on your belly; the other way is to kick them in the teeth."[18]

Other explanations of British party cohesion also have been offered. For example, based on comparison between Britain and the United States, Epstein has suggested the demands of parliamentary government and the absence of strong local ties as additional sources of cohesion.[19] These explanations appear far less satisfying, however, when comparison is made with Italy instead. In this case, parliamentary government has not produced cohesion beyond perfunctory unity on most (but not all) divisions. While party unity may be necessary for cabinet stability in a parliamentary system, there is no immutable law that cabinets must be stable. In fact, one major source of cabinet instability in Italy has been withdrawal of support by a faction within the ruling party. Localism and sectionalism in Britain appear of minor importance when compared with the United States. But in comparison to countries like Italy with far less cohesive parties, the problems posed by Welsh and Scottish nationalism, not to mention the local attachments of Yorkshire, Cornwall, Devon, or Northern Ireland, are quite significant.

That American parties are not cohesive may be explained in part by the federal structure of American government. The president is the only official elected in a national contest. While Congress is the national legislature, since the founding of the Republic it has been as much an assembly of state delegations as an arena in which two national parties do battle. Most elected officials, most political money, and most patronage positions are involved in state politics. It is in many ways fair to say that America has fifty two-party systems, not one. Naturally, this inhibits national party cohesion, although there is somewhat more cohesion within the state delegations. Even these, however, are cohesive only in comparison to the national organizations, a relative cohesion best explained by coincidence of opinion and self-interest among people from the same area of the country. Further, many state legislative parties are no more cohesive than their congressional counterparts. Moreover, federalism has not had the same impact on the unity of Canadian or German parties.

The direct primary is often cited as another cause of fragmentation in American parties. The primary simultaneously obliges politicians to maintain individual campaign organizations for the purpose of mounting or repelling intraparty challenges while freeing "forces driving toward the disintegration of party organizations. . . . The convention system compelled leaders to treat, to deal, to allocate nominations; the primary permits individual aspirants by one means or another to build a wider following within the party."[20] Although the direct primary is not unique to the United States,[21] it is unusual enough to preclude argument with this explanation by counter example. Clearly this means that the direct primary per se cannot be a necessary condition of fragmentation.

Many attempts have been made to explain the degree to which Japanese parties, and particularly the Liberal Democratic party (LDP), deviate from the norm of cohesion. Election of the party leader, assignment of cabinet posts, nomination of candidates, and even the awarding of government contracts and the choice of retirement careers are strongly influenced by factional affiliations. At the same time, while the LDP attracts, among both leaders and followers, adherents of a wide range of policy preferences, these preferences are only weakly related to factional structure, notwithstanding the fact that the winner of the interfactional struggle determines national policy.

Thayer suggests five stimuli to the formation of factions within the LDP.[22] The first, to which he attaches the greatest importance, is the selection of the party leader, and therefore the prime minister, by intraparty election. Since the number of electors is only about 500, personal arrangements may be made and factions, he suggests, reflect deals between would-be prime ministers and their followers in which money, status, and access to office are exchanged for votes. However, while this system, instituted as a condition of the merger of the Liberal and Democratic parties in 1955, may have led to the crystallization of the previously existing factions, both of the LDP's parent parties were factionalized even though their leaders "emerged." Further, British party leaders are elected by an even more restricted electorate, and are just as certain of the premiership when their parties are in power, yet this has not led to the same sort of factionalism in Britain.

Thayer's second stimulus is the importance of money in Japanese politics. The average cost per candidate of Japanese campaigns is over $40,000, and while expenditures in excess of $100,000 are not rare, the most a candidate reasonably can expect from the party is about $11,000. The factional leader provides funds and, more importantly, access to major contributors, in exchange for the support of his followers. But if money is important in Japanese politics, it traditionally has been even more important in American politics. If the American candidate's need for money has not led to party cohesion, neither has it led to factionalism. While the distribution of mobilizable money and the ways in which it may be secured are likely to play important roles in determining behavior (see below), it is not clear that the need for funds by itself has much explanatory power.

The third stimulus is the competition within the LDP for posts in the cabinet, the party, and the Diet. The factions operate as parties within the party, as members organize behind a leader in order to increase their bargaining power. As with the election of the party leader, however, the same situation is faced by British parliamentarians, yet Japanese style party factions have not emerged.

Fourth, Thayer suggests the Japanese electoral system as a cause of disunity. Members of the Diet are chosen by the system of plurality election from multimember districts with each voter given a single nontransferable ballot.[23] Thus, candidates are in direct electoral competition with their copartisans, and indeed to the extent that partisanship constrains the party vote totals, this is the only competition there is. By this interpretation, the factions serve as parties within the party in the competition for individual votes in general elections. This system is unique, so counter examples are impossible. The argument is, however, remarkably similar to those made about the American direct primary or the Italian system of preference voting.[24]

Finally, Thayer indicates a number of psychological motivations for factionalism. While many of these, for example "the desire to be in on all the political drama," may help explain the continuance of factions, they do not explain their origins. Most of these motivations, like the need for an object of identification or the desire to be an insider, are common to all politicians in all countries and so are of little help in explaining national differences.

This brief, and obviously spotty, review suggests a common problem and a common thread. The common problem stems from the case study approach. As isolated hypotheses, virtually all of the suggestions recited above are subject to refutation by counter example. Only when the supposed cause was unique could this not be done, but this means only that the hypothesis is nonfalsifiable, not that it is correct. Case studies, and indeed all inductive studies based on system level variables, suffer from a "degrees of freedom" problem in that the number of possible explanations far exceeds the number of cases.[25] While either may be used to help verify an independently constructed theory or to suggest a new theory, a hypothesis cannot validly be derived and tested with the same data. In their specifics, many of the hypotheses above fall into the trap of the "most peculiar feature" approach, saying in effect, "Here is a deviation from what theory suggests should be the case; there is the most peculiar cultural (or social or economic) trait of the country; therefore the trait must be the cause of the deviation."

The common thread is far more important. All these hypotheses ultimately rest on the centrality of careerist self-interest in determining how politicians behave. In detail, each emphasizes factors that are unique to a single country, and therefore cannot be generalized beyond it. Overall, however, the underlying force that gives each of these arguments its power is the desire of politicians to be elected to parliament, and once elected to retain their seats and to advance within the parliamentary party. Control over nominations, the operation of the electoral system, the need for financial or interest group support, are all important because they are central to the problem of election. The effects of institutional similarities and differences, seemingly inexplicable in isolation, are readily understandable when taken in conjunction with other environmental factors and applied specifically to the problem of election or intraparty advancement.

Theories or hypotheses of this type are clearly within the "economic approach" as defined by Brian Barry, or what Holt and Richardson called the "rationalistic paradigm."[26] While most of the authors cited above do not work entirely within this paradigm, their work certainly reflects its flavor. The word *paradigm* is used to refer to a group of theories sharing a common underlying view of the nature of the universe—the basic components that comprise it and the forces motivating them. A paradigm is thus a theory about theories. Although workers within the same paradigm may disagree in the particular assumptions they make, they are distinguished from adherents of other paradigms by their agreement on what the assumptions should be about and the form they should take. They agree on what a good theory would look like, even if they do not all hold the same specific theory.

The assumptions of a paradigm are not sufficient for empirical conclusions to be deduced, since they are assumptions about theories and not about the world. To go beyond this, additional assumptions must be made, and in doing so one moves from the level of paradigmatic thinking to the level of theory. Theories may be either very general or very specific; they may attempt to explain all behavior or only one minor phenomenon, depending on the range of their empirical assumptions. Middle range theory is clearly possible within any paradigm, but no coherent theory is possible at any level of generality without an overarching notion of how behavior in general is to be explained.

Likewise, within a given paradigm there can be more than one theory about the same phenomenon, since the empirical assumptions on which the theories are based may differ. Precisely because they are founded on empirical assumptions, two theories within the same paradigm cannot both be correct; either they are both special cases of some more general theory or else at least one is wrong. On the other hand, different theories in different paradigms may be simultaneously valid because at root they are theories about different things. Empirical disconfirmation of a theory disconfirms its empirical assumptions, not the paradigm from which it is drawn. A paradigm is undermined by being shown not useful—as might be the case if no theory within its umbrella could be confirmed or if all such theories were unreasonably complex—rather than untrue.

The theory to be presented in the following chapter is intended to apply to the world of the rationalistic paradigm. This world is quite simple and familiar. It is made up of consciously self-interested rational actors. Consciously self-interested actors are individuals who perceive that they have interests and are able to act on the basis of those interests. People are actors of this type. So might be political parties or organized interest groups, although more properly one would say that in some contexts parties or groups behave like self-interested actors and so may be treated as such for analytic simplicity. Even then they remain collections of discrete people whose cooperation must be explained, and they may be considered as actors in rationalistic theories only to the extent that they can take collective action.[27] Thus, what group theorists refer to as "latent groups" do not exist in the world of rationalistic theory.

Rationality implies that in deciding whether and how to act, these individuals always attempt to maximize the rewards obtained from a given input, or to minimize the input for a given level of gratification. Rational actors are not assumed to be omniscient; indeed, the cost of obtaining information may be an important element in the calculation, and a rational actor may decide that a blind guess offers a higher expected return than the decision possible only after an expensive investment in fact-finding. Neither is the rational actor always assumed to be right; one may make rational choices on the basis of misinformation. All that is required is that the best information available at a reasonable cost be used to achieve the actor's goals, whatever they may be, as cheaply as possible.[28] Starting with this basic world view, rationalistic theories attempt to explain behavior by showing deductively that if actors were rational then they would behave as they are known really to behave. Stopping here, one would not have said much, for it seems apparent that all behavior is rational. One does not find it illuminating to say, "He did what he did because he wanted to." Indeed, if one counts the desire to avoid discomfort as a valid end, even a psychotic's withdrawal from reality must be adjudged rational.[29] Rationalist theories advance beyond this by making additional assumptions about the ends that people pursue and thus arrive at simplified models of reality from which nonobvious conclusions may be deduced. But at this level, one leaves the general world of the rationalistic paradigm and descends to the level of a particular theory.

Working within the rationalistic paradigm commits one to the assumption that actors are rational in the pursuit of their goals. The additional central assumption of the theory of this book is that the members of legislative parties are motivated primarily by the desire to secure their own reelection. The parliamentary party itself is the result of their efforts. Is the assumption of electoral motivation reasonable? As has been observed, the defining characteristic of a parliamentary party is the fact that its members have been successful in the electoral arena. In order to remain members of the legislative party, individual politicians must continue to be successful electorally. The relatively small number of voluntary retirements among parliamentarians, their generally long tenure in office, and the effort and expense they incur to secure election attest to the strength of their motivation. Even if simple membership in the party is not the ultimate aim of politicians, but merely a means to some other end such as policy modification, status, or power, reelection is a prerequisite to the continued use of that means.[30]

It should be stressed that the empirical assumption is that politicians behave *as if* they were rationally calculating the most effective means of securing reelection. In constructing and testing a theory, one is working simultaneously in two distinct worlds, the real world of everyday experience and a hypothetical model of that world. The hope is that the behaviors of real world actors, which one would like to explain or predict, will correspond to those of the hypothetical actors in the model.[31] This hoped for behavioral isomorphism does not require identical logical processes. Thus, it need not be assumed that politicians consciously make calculations in anything like the style employed here. Decisions on the basis of rules of thumb, folk wisdom, or respected advice are consistent with the assumption of rationality if there is reason to believe that they are the same decisions that would have resulted from formal calculations.[32] Since these calculations are intended to produce the most effective strategy in a highly competitive situation, the obvious success of most incumbents in securing reelection gives good grounds to believe that, for whatever reason, "they must be doing something right."[33]

The specific objective of this book is to explain the issue orientation, ideological style, and structural coherence (cohesion versus disintegration versus factionalism) of legislative parties. In doing this, the party is seen as an agglomeration of individual politicians, structured to reflect their reelection needs and strategies. The goal of these politicians, reelection, is an assumption. The strategies that would be adopted by a rational candidate in pursuit of this goal are determined by the environment in which that pursuit takes place. Strategies appropriate to one environment may well be counterproductive in another. Clearly this set of variables must figure prominently in any rationalistic explanation of behavior. As conceived here, electoral environment is made up of two main elements—the electoral system and the distribution of politically mobilizable resources.

Rational strategies are determined in part by the electoral system in force. One element of this system is the electoral law. As the rules governing the opportunity to become a candidate, permissible types of campaign activity, and the ultimate translation of votes into parliamentary seats, these laws both limit behavior and determine how the score of the electoral game is kept. Since different electoral systems will reward the same distribution of votes differently, they may be expected to have an immediate impact on the calculations of politicians. Further, experience with the actual operation of the electoral system as conditioned by electoral behavior and with norms established by custom rather than by statute also plays a role in defining the electoral environment. For example, a widespread preference for local candidates may be as significant as a constitutional requirement of residence within one's constituency.[34]

Mounting an effective campaign requires the mobilization of many resources, among them money, organization, and workers. Both the relative importance of these resources and the manner in which they are distributed may vary widely from one setting to another. Nonetheless, all candidates are faced with the problem of acquiring the means with which to pursue the strategies that the electoral system alone might dictate. Since the strategy best suited to resource mobilization may not complement that best suited to campaigning among the electorate at large, compromise frequently will be necessary. As a result, any attempt to explain or predict politicians' behavior, and through that the nature of parliamentary parties, must take the distribution of politically relevant resources into account.

What follows is an attempt to explain differences among parliamentary parties by developing a deductive theory that allows party structure to be predicted from a description of the electoral environment. How is the success or failure of this explanation to be judged? This is clearly a specific case of the problem of judging the success of any deductive theory of politics. The standard of proof most often suggested by those who propose these theories is their predictive accuracy. Downs, for example, says that "Theoretical models should be tested primarily by the accuracy of their predictions."[35] He is certainly not the only one to claim a fundamental identity between prediction and explanation.[36] A theory whose predictions are wrong in most cases is obviously of little value. On the other hand, prediction by itself is a very weak test. In the first place, given the limited number of cases and virtually infinite number of possible explanations, several theories will be equally accurate. How can one pick the one that is actually best? Second, since all theories are based on oversimplification—extracting a few variables to which primacy is assigned and ignoring all others—no theory less complex than reality will be perfectly accurate. Finally, the prediction of the obvious is not a strong standard of test, and that is precisely what rationalistic theories do. Indeed, it is what they are intended to do. Starting with a well known fact—for example that most people avoid voting for a third party in single-member plurality elections, or that many people will not join a trade union unless forced to do so by a union or closed shop—the theorist attempts to explain, not predict. To be sure, a successful theory may lead to nonobvious predictions, and their validity provides partial confirmation of the theory, but this is not the primary utility of this type of work.

For a theory to be useful in explanation, it must meet two further requirements. First, it must be based on assumptions that seem reasonable. One would not rate highly a theory explaining the damage done at a fire on the basis of the number of engines called to the scene, notwithstanding the theory's predictive accuracy.[37] Rather, intuitive notions of how the world works lead one to consider this to be a spurious correlation; one says that both variables are determined by the intensity of the fire. The central assumption of the theory to be presented in this book is that politicians tend to behave, whether by accident or design, in ways that an informed observer would consider rational if their primary goal were reelection. The reasonableness of this assumption already has been argued; clearly unless its reasonableness is accepted, nothing that follows may be seen as other than coincidence.

As already suggested, the world of a theory is in effect a model of reality. For a model to be useful in explanation, it must be like the thing modeled not only in result, but also in the method by which that result is reached. From this is derived the second additional requirement for successful explanation, that the intermediate steps by which the final prediction is reached be themselves empirically accurate.[38] The more specific predictions that can be verified, the more confidence may be placed in the theory that generated them.

The overall plan of this book is based on Sherlock Holmes's famous dictum that in trying to deduce how things happened one should "think backwards." From the point of view of the candidate, an election may be seen as having three semidistinct phases: nomination, campaigning, and the actual balloting and determination of the winners. Logically, this temporal sequence is reversed. Campaigning is constrained by the fact that it is an attempt to influence the outcome of the balloting, while the nomination stage likewise is constrained by the fact that nomination is only valuable if it permits the mounting of an effective campaign. Since the most productive tactics for each stage of the electoral process are determined by the requirements of the stages that follow, presentation will begin at the end with the impact of four aspects of electoral law, and work backwards from there through the operation of the resulting electoral systems, campaigning, and nominations.

In the context of the rationalistic paradigm in particular, and theorizing in the social sciences in general, deductions rarely have the rigor of a mathematical proof. Although Riker's size principle is proven in a formal sense, for example, the rest of his argument and conclusions are not.[39] Likewise, a true purist might call the work of Downs and of Olsen persuasive argumentation rather than deduction. In fact, strict logical deduction rarely has been attempted in political science, and then (with a few exceptions in the field of formal voting theory) usually with disappointing results. On the other hand, the difference is very great between more loosely deductive theory, in which arguments are based on explicitly stated assumptions and conclusions are derived from them, and inductive theory, in which conclusions are generalizations from oberservation. The theory developed in this book is intended to be of the deductive type. As is the case with other work in this field, purists may find some of the deductions less than pristine in form.

Clearly the reasonableness and persuasiveness of the assumptions and arguments must be judged by the reader. Two bodies of data will be analyzed to demonstrate the predictive accuracy of the theory. The overall predictions based on electoral law alone will be tested with the data for forty-nine parties in fourteen Western democracies gathered by the International Comparative Political Parties (ICPP) project.[40]

Full investigation of many predictions requires more detailed information than is available in the ICPP data, or indeed than reasonably could be obtained for such a large number of parties. To test these, six parties, two from each of three European countries, were studied intensively. These parties are the Labour and Conservative parties in Great Britain, Fianna Fail and Fine Gael in the Republic of Ireland, and the Democrazia Cristiana and Partito Socialista Italiano in Italy. In addition to the information gathered from an extensive reading of the literature on these countries, data were gathered from interviews with a sample of deputies, defeated candidates, and local officials of each party. Sampling information and a typical form of the questionnaire used are given in Appendix A and Appendix B, respectively. Two parties were included for each country to control for the effect of party rather than electoral environment; within the limits discussed in later chapters, the theory suggests that all parties within a single electoral environment should have the same structure. The countries chosen offer a variety of electoral and sociocultural environments in which to test hypotheses. Nonetheless, if the sample is in a sense representative, it is neither random nor large, and conclusions based on it must be regarded as illustrations, rather than as definitive proof. The reader is encouraged to test the theory further by considering the predictions that would be made for other parties of which he or she has detailed knowledge.

2

Electoral Law

ELECTORAL law plays a central role in the theory to be developed here. The motivating assumption is that the principal, and certainly the immediate, object of each parliamentary candidate is to be successful personally in securing a legislative seat. Rationality takes on relevance because there are normally more aspirants to parliamentary office than there are mandates to be distributed. Likewise, a candidate's success or failure in securing election provides the standard by which the efficacy of his overall campaign performance must be judged. As a result, strategy at each earlier stage in a candidate's quest for office must be decided at least in part on the basis of the requirements of, and the opportunities created or foreclosed by, the formal electoral system. Thus, the nature of the choice that voters are allowed to make and the way in which their decisions in the form of votes are translated into a list of elected deputies must be kept firmly in mind if one hopes to understand nominating and campaign practices, to identify the important elements of the overall electoral environment, and ultimately to explain the nature of the resulting parliamentary parties.

The empirical expectation underlying the theory is that the answer to the following question will describe the structure of real parties: "If rational candidates were designing a party with no aim in mind other than maximizing their own chances of election and reelection, what would it be like?" Electoral law influences party structure because candidates, as individuals attempting to maximize their chances of victory, pattern their behavior in ways determined by those laws. Conversely, the parties, as organizations and agents of successful candidates, have their structures controlled by the electoral needs of the candidates they serve. In particular, from the point of view of a candidate, the provisions of the electoral law are important because they influence the "correct" answers to three questions central to the determination of a rational electoral strategy. First, which voters should the candidate try hardest to influence? Second, what should he try to influence them to do? Third, what is the most effective way of appealing to them? The problem for this chapter is to deduce the implications of electoral law for the rational answers to these questions, and the probable impact of those answers on party organizations.

Ultimately, the success or failure of candidates is measured by their ability to influence voters. This means that no answers to the three questions about strategy just posed, and hence no conclusions about likely party structure, can be reached without some assumptions about the way voters make up their minds and the nature of the political universe in which they do so. The bulk of this chapter will be devoted to a detailed analysis of the probable impact of a number of specific aspects of electoral law. Before returning to this, however, it is necessary to introduce the assumptions about voters and electoral competition on which the analysis will be predicated. Specifically, it is assumed that:

1. Electoral competition may be modeled adequately as taking place in an n-dimensional policy space, where n is greater than or equal to two.

The dimensions will be referred to here as issues, but may represent personality evaluations, ethnic or geographic ties, partisan loyalties, and so forth, in addition to specific questions of public policy. Where *issues* refers only to policy questions, this should be clear from the context. While the term *issues,* as used, here, refers to mutually independent dimensions, this should not be confused with an assumption that each policy stand articulated by the parties is completely unrelated to all the others and to personality, ethnic, or other considerations. All that is required by this assumption is that each of these concerns ("issues" in common language, but not issues as defined here) may be modeled as a combination of positions on independent dimensions.[1]

2. At any given election, there is a fixed and finite number of parties competing in the nation as a whole, although the number and identity of the parties competing in each constituency may vary within this constraint.

3. In each constituency, the disutility to a party resulting from the loss of a previously held seat is greater than the utility gain of winning a new seat.

The latter assumption should make particular sense if it is remembered that the loss of a previously held seat is likely to involve the defeat of an incumbent deputy. Since the party is assumed to be primarily an organization of incumbents seeking their own electoral success, this form of conservatism follows directly. Moreover, incumbents not only are valuable to their parties by virtue of their experience, but also are likely to be in a position to do considerable harm to the party (and its other candidates) if their interests are sacrificed unduly.

4. Each party choses one point in the policy space, corresponding to a unique combination of issue positions, so as to maximize its

expected utility (that is, the sum of the expected utilities of its members), in conformity with assumption 3.

Thus the party already has selected the most advantageous platform at the time when these deductions begin and no further changes should be anticipated during the campaign.[2] Each party has only one national platform, and while candidates in different districts may emphasize different aspects of that platform, or appeal to voters in different ways, all candidates of the party are committed to the same platform position.[3] Deviations from the party platform are punished by the voters in accordance with assumption 8.

5. Each voter most prefers the combination of policies corresponding to one point in the policy space and ranks the parties according to her perception of the distances between their platforms and her most preferred point. (The conclusions to be presented below follow whether this distance is measured by a Euclidean or a "city-block" metric; all illustrations will be based on a Euclidean metric.)[4] While voters may change their preferences over time, these changes will be gradual. At each particular time, small changes in preferences are more likely than large changes.

6. Turnout is influenced by the voter's perceptions of the impact of their votes relative to their own preferences. Turnout thus will be lower for voters whose most preferred policy points are far from all parties competing in their district and for voters whose most preferred points are roughly equidistant from all parties competing.

Clearly, the latter condition is likely to be met only when there are exactly two parties competing.

7. Voters are distributed among districts so the the distribution of preferences with respect to parties are not the same in all constituencies. Simply, there is regional diversity in political preferences.

8. Any appeal made by a candidate will be perceived by all voters and compared to his party's platform. Inconsistency between appeals made by a candidate and the party's platform will undermine electoral confidence in the candidate and the party. This will reduce the turnout of their voters and their ability to attract marginal supporters and campaign-relevant resources, thus reducing their total vote.

While turnout effects naturally will be minimized where voting is compulsory, it should be noted that even in those countries in which voting is mandatory there can be marginal fluctuations in turnout and in the frequency of spoiled or blank ballots.[5]

Having thus defined the main behavioral characteristics of electoral competition as it is assumed to exist, attention can return to the impact of electoral law. Here, some simplification is clearly necessary. The full electoral law of a country includes innumerable details vital to the administration of elections without necessarily being of strategic importance to candidates: forms of evidence acceptable as proof of citizenship; the location of polling places and the hours during which they will be open; the identity of the officials empowered to count the ballots and certify the result. From this tangle, one must select those aspects of electoral law that are of the greatest importance. Initial guidance in this task may be taken from Rae's classic study of the political consequences of electoral laws. Rae dealt with three basic dimensions: the electoral formula; whether the voter's choice is categoric or ordinal; and the average size of districts.[6] Since Rae's concern was with the aggregate success of parties, while this theory focuses attention on individual candidates, a fourth dimension, the existence of an intraparty electoral choice, must be added. As will be seen below, each of these four dimensions relates directly to one or more of the strategic questions posed earlier: which voters a rational candidate should appeal to, what he should try to influence them to do, and how most effectively to appeal to them. Through answers to these questions, the four dimensions relate in turn to the kind of party rational candidates would be expected to form.

Electoral Formula

The first of Rae's dimensions to be considered, the electoral formula, is particularly relevant in determining the voters to whom the candidate should appeal, and because of that in determining the kind of appeal that is most likely to be effective. This dimension concerns the way in which the votes are counted and translated into a division of seats among parties. While there are virtually as many specific schemes by which this may be done as there are countries holding elections, schemes may be divided roughly into two classes: plurality election and proportional representation (PR). For the most part, it is immediately apparent to which class any particular system belongs. The quintessential plurality systems, like those of the United States or Great Britain, use single-member plurality elections, or the "first past the post" system. Here candidates present themselves as individuals, either with or without the benefit of party backing and either with or without party affiliation identified on the ballot. There is one position to be filled and each voter casts a single ballot. The one candidate who receives the most votes is elected, whether or not he had a majority and regardless of how well his opponents may have done. This process is repeated simultaneously in as many separate constituencies as there are parliamentary mandates to be distributed.

At the opposite extreme are systems like the Israeli one, in which the entire country serves as the only constituency in a proportional system.

Candidates stand only as members of party lists, and it is for one or another of these lists that the elector's ballot actually is cast. The total number of seats to be awarded then is divided among the parties in proportion to the number of votes received by them.

These extremes differ in three important respects. Most obviously, proportional representation systems are just that, proportional. The relationship between the proportion of the votes received by a party and the proportion of the seats awarded to it is very close in large district PR systems, and not very close at all in many single-member plurality systems.[7] In large measure, however, the relationship between proportionality of result and electoral formula is spurious, resulting rather from the fact that plurality election generally takes place in single-member districts while PR requires multimember districts. As Rae has shown, it is district magnitude, in terms of the number of deputies per district, that primarily determines the level of proportionality. In multimember plurality systems, a far higher degree of proportionality in outcome is achieved than in systems electing only one deputy from each district.

Of greater importance is the fact that in plurality systems one votes for candidates as individuals, while under PR one votes for groups of candidates, or lists. Finally, because the object of voting in plurality systems is the individual and because each candidate must be declared either elected or defeated, plurality schemes must be concerned with the order in which candidates finish rather than with the absolute numbers or percentages of votes received. There is, after all, no way to be proportional among individuals, each of whom must be either completely elected or else completely defeated. Rather than the statistical fairness of the outcome, these concerns with order (as the very word *plurality* implies) and with individuality are what most clearly distinguish plurality from proportional electoral formulae.

How does the distinction between plurality and PR formulae determine the most likely objects for a candidate's campaign efforts? Under any electoral system a candidate may expect to be better off when his party has more votes and the opponents' parties have fewer, but given an initial distribution of voter preferences, different systems reward or punish transfers of votes from one party to another differently. Looking first at PR systems, it is clear that under these formulae only the absolute percentage of the vote received by the candidate's party is important. In particular, in a perfectly proportional system, every transfer of votes to the candidate's party from another would be of equal value, as would be every transfer of votes going in the other direction be equally costly; transfers solely among other parties would have no impact on the candidate's electoral fortunes since they would not alter his party's share of the total vote. Under these circumstances, the rational candidate would try hardest to influence those voters who are most likely to change their votes to his party while attempting to defend the party's vote against those other parties that are most likely to be able to woo it away. Simultaneously, he must attempt to influence the party's supporters to vote rather than to abstain.

In fact, not all transfers of votes to a candidate's party are of equal value because no PR system can be perfectly proportional. Nonetheless, when the number of deputies to be returned from each district is reasonably large, deviations from perfect proportionality become effectively random, and rational candidates should react as if each transfer of votes were equally valuable. Since, by assumption, voters rank their preferences among parties according to the distances between the party platforms and their own most preferred positions in the policy space, the parties against which a candidate should most directly focus his campaign are those most directly competing for the same voters, that is, the voters who are roughly equidistant between the two parties.[8] These are the voters whose opinions would have to be changed the least in order to produce electoral change, and thus it is particularly to these voters that the candidate must appeal.

Now that the most likely objects for the campaign of a candidate competing in a PR system have been identified, what implications does this have for the content of his campaign? To answer this question requires a four-step argument. First, the identity of the parties against which the candidate should focus attention must be elaborated upon. Second, the likely number and distribution of these parties must be considered. Third, the pattern of competition that ought to result from this situation must be outlined. Only then can the strategy most appropriate for this pattern of competition be established.

If parties could be portrayed as occupying positions on a unidimensional issue line with each voter selecting the party nearest her most preferred position on that line, then those parties occupying adjoining positions would be in the most direct competition precisely because they would be the least different. In terms of an issue line, voters are far less likely to change their preferences to such an extent as to skip over a party than they are to shift between two adjacent,i.e., similar, parties. Likewise, differences in perception of party positions are most likely to affect votes for adjacent parties. In a multidimensional space, such as has been assumed here, a party might be seen to erect a metaphorical "circle" or "sphere of defense" around its position. For example, if Figure 2.1 represents the placement of seven parties in a two-dimensional issue space, party *B* will find itself most directly in conflict with parties *A, C,* and *G,* and it is against the candidates of these parties that the candidates of party *B* should concentrate their efforts. In other words, each candidate should focus his campaign against those parties that are most like his own.

FIG. 2.1.
Placement of seven parties in a hypothetical
two-dimensional issue space

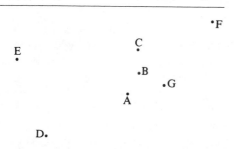

The specific number and location of these parties will, of course, vary from one system to another. Some more general conclusions about their number and distribution may be derived, however. Coupled with the fact that a party's most direct electoral enemies are those other parties whose platforms are closest to its own, is the well-known tendency of PR and large districts to encourage multiparty competition within each district while discouraging purely local minor party candidacies.[9] When these tendencies are taken with the fixed number of parties, two deductions may be made. First, under PR a party may expect to have more than one optimal enemy in each district.[10] In one dimension, this must be the case for all parties except for those at the two ends of the resulting party ordering. In general, when more than one dimension is required to represent party positions, all parties will have at least two optimal enemies in each district.[11] Second, looking across constituencies, it is likely that parties will have the same optimal enemies in different districts, since local candidates are discouraged while national parties are encouraged to compete in every district by the expectation that even small numbers of votes will be rewarded. While the identity, number, and location of a party's optimal enemies is specific to its particular system, in general one can conclude that it will have more than one, and the same, optimal enemies throughout the country.

From the first of these conclusions it follows that among a party's optimal campaign targets, i.e., those voters roughly equidistant between it and one of its optimal enemies, there will be two sets pulling the party in diametrically opposing directions. This is illustrated for the case of five parties in two dimensions in Figure 2.2. The solid lines map the "borders" between the "territories" of two parties in the space. Clearly any movement by a party to increase its vote by moving its platform closer to one of these borders also must cost it votes by moving the platform farther from another border.[12] One consequence of this is that several dimensions will be of importance in appealing to a party's optimal target voters in each district. But since each party's optimal enemies are likely to be the same in every district, it follows that not only several dimensions, but the same, or nearly the same, dimensions will be important in all constituencies.

Now, what about campaign strategy? In turn, these results lead to the expectation that rational candidates competing under PR will stress in their campaigns the virtue of their party's entire platform taken as a whole, and will appeal on the basis of proximity to that point. This is because candidates cannot ignore any relevant dimension for fear of losing voters whose preference for their party is based on that dimension. As has just been shown, however, many, if not all, dimensions are relevant in each district. Further, candidates must take a defensive stand. They must be more concerned with keeping their share of the electorate than with attempting to win new voters since any appeal to one group of marginal voters, which may be countered by the threatened party, risks the loss of marginal voters with relatively opposing views. Since the risk of possible losses has been assumed to outweigh the value of possible gains, there should be no tendency of moderate parties competing in PR systems to converge.[13] Instead, each party will stress the importance of the relatively small differences separating it from its most direct electoral competitors.[14]

From this it follows that parties competing in PR systems will tend to be ideological in their approach. Stressing relatively small differences in platforms is made easier if candidates may point to the putative consistency of one platform versus the inconsistency of another. Further, the problem of dealing with many issue dimensions simultaneously is simplified if issues may be related to a few underlying principles rather than being considered individually. Moreover, since candidates in different districts are facing roughly the same situations, consistency may be assured more readily by appeal to general principles imposing coherence over a variety of questions than by serial agreement on a great number of separate issues. This way of organizing one's arguments, however, is the very definition of ideological thought.[15]

In contrast, plurality electoral systems act to encourage single issue campaigns, or campaigns based on personality or locality. This is made particularly clear if the same line of reasoning just employed for proportional systems is retraced for plurality elections. (The same results follow for multimember constituencies if the additional assumption is granted that candidates act to increase the number of candidates of their party elected. The argument here will be presented in terms of single-member plurality election. The problem of intraparty conflict, which might entail the violation of this additional assumption in multimember plurality systems, is discussed below.)

Under PR each party is rewarded with seats in proportion to its share of

FIG. 2.2.
Territories of five parties in a two-dimensional issue space
(mapped by solid lines) with demonstration that each must appeal
to voters with diametrically opposing interests

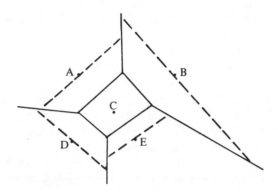

the votes. Hence its candidates may be expected always to be attempting to maximize that share in the easiest way possible. Therefore, they should focus their campaigns against the parties whose platforms are most similar to their own. Under a plurality scheme, however, a party need only be concerned with the order in which it finishes. As a result, not all transfers of votes are equally valuable or costly to a party's candidate, nor have transfers in general the same value to all parties. This means that the value of votes received, as well as the ease of acquiring them, must enter a candidate's identification of his party's optimal enemies, so that these enemies may not be those nearest the candidate's own party in the issue space. Moreover, as will be seen below, the optimal enemies of the candidate's party need not be the same in every district. Thus, neither of the conditions promoting ideological conflict under PR systems is met under plurality schemes.

In a plurality system, the candidates in any district may be divided with rough accuracy into two categories—*ceteris paribus*, those that are expected to be successful and those that are expected to be defeated. The farther a candidate lies from the line dividing these two classes, whether above or below, the less likely he is to turn defeat into victory or victory into defeat, and consequently the less interest the candidate and his party need have in the campaign. Further, since the only relevant question is the side of this line on which a candidate is found, transfers between candidates on opposite sides are far more valuable or costly than transfers between two expected winners or two expected losers, although even here the value of the transfer would depend strongly on the distance between the two. In the single-member case of particular concern here, this means that the most valuable transfers are those occurring between the strongest candidate and his closest competitor. Thus, the most intense and important conflict in each single-member district should occur between the top two parties. Third parties may be expected to have difficulty attracting interest, resources, or voters, leading to the well-known tendency of single-member plurality elections to produce two-party competition at the district level.[16]

The differing values of votes depend on what parties they are coming from or going to. This phenomenon may be illustrated by a simple example. Suppose three parties competing in a single-member district currently share the vote in a ratio of 48:46:6. Then, the party in the middle can afford to lose 1.5 votes to the small party for every vote it gains from the big party until, having gained just over 4 percent from one side while losing just over 6 percent to the other, it moves into first place.

In contrast to the multiplicity of optimal enemies confronting each party under PR, in a single-member plurality system, each party will have only one optimal enemy in each constituency. Moreover, since the rankings of the parties differ across district lines, with the top two parties the main focus of competition in each district, a party will have different optimal enemies in different districts. This expectation is furthered by the fact that plurality systems encourage local candidates, so that some parties may be competing in only a few districts.[17]

Since a party has only one optimal enemy in each district, only a few issue dimensions are likely to be relevant in each, and just as the identity of the optimal enemy may vary across districts so may the issues that are important. This is illustrated in Figures 2.3 and 2.4, which contrast a party's situation under a plurality system with its situation under PR. Figure 2.3 maps the territory of one of four parties competing under PR, where the party may expect to face all three other parties in each constituency. In Figures 2.4a through 2.4c, the party's territory is mapped under a plurality system where it may expect to be concerned with these parties only one at a time.

Because each party has only one optimal enemy per constituency, it is not pulled in opposite directions by two sets of voters among its optimal electoral targets. This is immediately clear if Figures 2.2 and 2.4 are compared. Thus parties can try to minimize the apparent difference separating them. Instead of stressing the importance of relatively small differences, they should tend to minimize the importance of larger ones. This approach leads to an apparent or "dishonest" convergence of platforms, even when the actual platforms remain unchanged; frequently it leads to a real convergence over time as well.[18]

Under these circumstances, there should be no tendency toward an ideological political style. While the positions taken by each of party *B*'s

FIG. 2.3.
Placement of four parties in a hypothetical two-dimensional issue
space with the political territory of party *B* mapped under PR

___

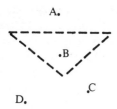

candidates in Figure 2.4 are consistent with the ideologically defined
position illustrated in Figure 2.3, commitment to the entire position would
be a distinct embarrassment to each of them. Just as votes are valued in
terms of more or less, rather than absolute numbers, so candidates will wish
to take relative, rather than absolute, issue positions. If redistribution of
income, for example, is an important issue, each candidate competing under
a plurality formula would be expected to stress only that he favored more or
less redistribution than his optimal enemy in the district. Candidates in PR
systems, however, ought to stress exactly how much redistribution they
favor since, in general, they will have to defend their share of the electorate
against parties that favor more distribution as well as against parties that
favor less. To do otherwise would encourage the abstention of extremist
supporters for whom, if a candidate's position is preferable to that of the

FIG. 2.4.
Placement of four parties in a hypothetical two-dimensional issue space with the political
territory of party *B* mapped in pairwise competition with each other party under
plurality election

___

a. Party *B* versus party *A*   b. Party *B* versus party *C*   c. Party *B* versus party *D*

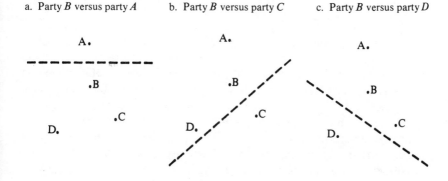

prime opponent, it is still not very desirable. At the same time, the candidate would allow opponents to capitalize on the ambiguity of such a relative position to attract voters from the contested region between them.

Reference to irrelevant dimensions is also counterproductive. Not only does it divert resources from the primary battleground, it also may increase the apparent distance between the candidate and some would-be supporters. The electoral chances of each candidate thus are improved if he takes a stand on a single issue and ignores all others.[19] To the extent that issues are important, plurality schemes encourage candidates to deal with them one at a time, referring only to those of local importance; general principles, which indirectly would commit candidates to positions on other dimensions or to consistent emphases across district lines, are to be avoided.

Before leaving the discussion of electoral formula, one additional link must be pointed out between PR and ideological parties on the one hand and plurality formulae and more flexible parties on the other. In PR systems, voters choose parties rather than individuals. Because candidates are obliged to say "Vote for my party" rather than "Vote for me," it is more difficult for candidates of the same party to take different political lines. The importance of the corporate identity of the party is increased, and particularly the importance of the sense that its issue stands represent a unified program rather than a number of isolated proposals of individual candidates. Correspondingly, the general organizing principles underlying specific proposals, that is the ideology, become more important.[20]

Conversely, plurality electoral schemes encourage personalistic or localistic campaigning. Since the choice of voters is for candidates rather than for parties, candidates may attempt to minimize or even ignore their party affiliation, and the commitment to a specific platform that this implies.[21] This naturally increases the relative importance of personality. Because local candidacies are encouraged, localistic considerations will be of particular importance to some candidates (facing a local party challenge) and of some importance to most candidates (hoping to prevent such a challenge in the future).

Nature of Choice

Rae's second dimension concerns the nature of the choice voters are allowed to express. In some electoral systems, voters make a simple choice among parties or candidates and the entire weight of each voter's ballot is given to the single individual or list chosen. Rae calls this a categoric choice. In other cases, however, the voter is allowed to express a more complex preference structure, either splitting her vote among parties or giving it to one party with provision that it may be transferred to another under certain circumstances. This Rae calls an ordinal choice. (The possibility of splitting one's vote among candidates of a single party is considered below. Here we are concerned only with interparty choice.) The distinction between ordinal and categoric choice bears heavily on the second of the candidate's questions, what should he try to convince the voters to do, and indirectly on the first question as well.

If the choice to be made by the voters is categoric, the candidate's approach with regard to other parties must be antagonistic. There can be no cooperation across party lines. In order to increase the party's strength, the candidate must try to convert the voters of opposing parties into voters for his own party. Under PR, alliances across party lines are of no value unless there is some disproportionate bonus awarded to parties or alliances with a certain minimum vote.[22] Under plurality schemes, two forms of alliance are possible: one party may withdraw to the benefit of another or a party may ally with a second by agreeing to enter the race to steal votes from some third party. In either case, however, once the list of contestants is established, the parties within each constituency must be antagonistic where only categoric choice is allowed. (It might be observed that the possibility of alliances of these types only increases the dissimilarity among a party's oppositions in different districts under plurality election.) Further, under either formula, parties allying run the substantial risk of finishing with fewer votes than the sum of their original electoral strengths, since their joint platform must be farther from the first preference of some voters than was the nearer of their individual platforms. Particularly under PR, where much is made of minor differences, the shaking of voters' preconceptions involved in changing a primary enemy into an ally may also lead to increased abstentions even among those voters who most prefer the combined platform position.

Where choice is ordinal, however, the candidate faces a more complex and ambiguous dilemma. The very parties with which his own is in the most direct conflict for first preference votes or for the lion's share of a split vote are the parties from which it is most likely that second preference, transfer, or partial votes will be received. While antagonistic actions toward these parties may encourage a few voters to switch parties, such actions at the same time may hurt the party's chances of receiving secondary support from a far larger number of voters. As a result, the candidate may be tempted to soften policy appeals and to bring such nonpartisan criteria as personality and locality (especially in plurality systems) to bear in order to attract second place votes. Alliances among parties are made possible since they may increase the frequency of transfers of second place votes among the allying parties without costing any of them first place votes. This too should tend to soften the differences among parties. Where ordinal choice is allowed, the intensity of conflict between parties should be minimized and the distinctions among them made more vague. Issues will tend to be less important as concerns that more readily allow appeals across party lines come to the fore. Categoric choice will tend to sharpen interparty conflict.

District Magnitude

The third dimension considered by Rae is district magnitude, operationalized as the average number of deputies returned per district. In fact, this is only one aspect of district size. Districts also vary tremendously with regard to the number of voters within them. Taken together, these two then determine a third aspect of district magnitude, the average number of voters represented by each deputy.[23] It is obviously a far different problem to campaign to 2,500 voters than it is to campaign to 250,000 or to campaign as the only candidate from a party rather than as one of several candidates from the same party (as would be the case in a multimember district). But precisely what difference should district magnitude make for candidates?

In districts with relatively few voters, the likelihood that a candidate will be known personally by a significant proportion of his constituents is naturally greater than in districts with many voters. Meeting large numbers of voters and appealing to them on the basis of personal acquaintance only becomes a viable strategy when the district population is reasonably small. Under these circumstances, appeal to locality also may be expected. As an empirical matter, these trends ought to be most common in rural and traditionally oriented areas, where localism and personalism are likely to be embedded in the political culture. On the other hand, as the population of a district grows, the proportion of the voters that can be known by a single candidate must shrink, and so this type of appeal must be supplemented with less direct appeals.

This difference may be multiplied by its interaction with the number of deputies per district. Assuming that the size of the legislature remains constant, multimember districts can be constructed only by increasing the number of voters in each one. This is likely to reduce the scope of personal and local appeals, as just discussed. In addition, multimember districts imply that each party will have more than one candidate per constituency. Under these circumstances, the personal visibility of each candidate is reduced and party becomes a more salient feature of electoral choice. Further, local appeals are less likely to be effective since each candidate can be the "local man" to a far smaller proportion of the voters. Although under these circumstances a party may be tempted to nominate a few candidates with strong local ties in order to increase its vote in a few areas, local ties are rarely enough to get any of these candidates elected.[24] Likewise, in small districts, patronage and the provision of particularistic services may be important campaign techniques. Where districts are large, however, it is unlikely that there will be sufficient "goods" available to influence significant numbers of voters on an individualistic basis. While patronage and constituency service are important in all systems, only with small districts are they likely to become dominating practices, since only then can individuals reasonably claim credit for any particular result.[25]

The mechanics as well as the strategy of campaigning are affected by district size. When there are few voters in a district, campaigning is likely to be conducted on a personal basis by the candidate and a few friends or loyal party workers. Fifty workers each contacting 100 people can speak personally to 5,000 voters. Not only is this approach less costly, it is also likely to be more effective provided that an adequate proportion of the electorate can be reached. When the candidate must reach tens or hundreds of thousands of voters, however, more reliance must be placed on campaigns through the media and by large numbers of volunteers or paid workers. In this case, the importance of organization (not necessarily formal party organization) and finance is greatly increased.

That there will be more parties competing in districts with many deputies than in districts with few follows directly from the payoff functions for all electoral systems; the more deputies there are to be elected in each district, the smaller the percentage of the vote necessary to win at least one seat. This allows appeals that will be popular with relatively narrow segments of the electorate, even if the individuals in question are geographically dispersed. In particular, it means that the differences in ideological style that result from PR versus plurality election will be greater for large district PR and small district plurality systems and less for small district PR or multimember plurality schemes.

Intraparty Electoral Choice

Under some systems, the division of the seats awarded to a party is left entirely to that party's discretion, although that discretion generally must be exercised before the election takes place. Under single-member systems, this is the case when the party is allowed to choose a single candidate without in any way consulting the voters at large. Under PR, the party might submit a list of candidates under the provision that its share of the constituency's seats will be awarded to candidates in the order in which their names appear on the list. In other systems, however, the particular candidates awàrded their party's share of the parliamentary seats may be selected totally or in part by the voters themselves. The American direct primary allows voters to choose the candidate who will compete under their party's banner in the general election. With PR, the order in which candidates are declared elected might be determined by a separate preference vote cast by electors choosing that party. The Japanese electoral system, discussed chapter 1, allows the voters to decide among a party's several candidates in a multimember plurality system. Obviously, many other devices are possible for allowing voters to choose personalities as well as parties. While Rae does not consider this dimension, it is of obvious importance for candidates interested in their own, not just their party's, chances of success.

When there is no opportunity for voters to express a relative preference among the candidates of a single party, the campaign for those candidates can be a cooperative venture. While some things may benefit one candidate more than another, perhaps even to the point of being exactly no help to some, there is nothing voters can do to aid one candidate while actually diminishing the electoral chance of another candidate of the same party. Regardless of how unfavorable a candidate's constituency or how unfavorable his position on the party list, the only way in which the candidate can increase his own chance of election is by increasing the party's total vote. Conversely, nothing that increases the party's vote can hurt him. In this case, a single campaign organization with unified control over tactics and resources within each district, or even over the entire nation, is likely to be the most effective way of advancing the fortunes of each candidate. In any event, there is no implicit conflict of interest to make such coordination impossible, and no incentive for one candidate of a party to attack another.

When voters not only determine the distribution of seats among parties, but also directly control the choice of particular candidates, however, this is distinctly not the case. While improving his party's overall vote may increase the probability that a particular candidate will be elected, it need not do so.[26] Moreover, at some point in the campaign each of the candidates must distinguish himself from his running mates and campaign against them for preference votes. This means that the candidate cannot conduct his entire campaign effectively through the party's organization; each must have an independent campaign machine, particularly interested in his election in addition to the general success of the party. Most importantly, each also must cultivate an independent source of whatever resources—funds, workers, group endorsements—are necessary to a successful campaign.[27]

The particular adaptations candidates make will then be determined by the distribution of mobilizable resources. Where these are dispersed, locally and personally oriented campaigns are to be expected as each candidate builds a personal machine. On the other hand, where control over electorally mobilizable resources is concentrated in the hands of a few individuals or organizations, it is more likely that candidates will form attachments within the party, cemented by dependence on a common patron.

The thrust of the theory presented here is that parliamentary party organization will appear as an extension of campaign organization, and hence will reveal the same structural characteristics as a rationally organized campaign. Thus, predictions of campaign organization based on the arguments presented above should also apply to the parliamentary party. Of course, the argument could equally be reversed. Perhaps politicians already organized in parliament construct electoral systems that will allow them to continue the same patterns of behavior outside parliament. Certainly, while the basic outlines of a country's electoral law were generally set when any particular politician first entered the political arena, electoral laws have been subject to major modifications over the course of 50 or 100 years. In either event, however, the basic theory remains the same—that rational behavior by politicians causes a coincidence of campaign and legislative organization. Beyond assessing the reasonableness of the deductions presented above, the test of the theory must come from examining this hypothesized empirical coincidence.

For many reasons that will be discussed at length in succeeding chapters, the real coincidence of rational campaign strategy and party organization will be less than perfect. One such reason that already has been alluded to is the possible muddling effects of electoral formula and district magnitude. Politicians competing in large district plurality systems or in small district PR systems will be pulled one way by one factor and the other way by the other. Nonetheless, in concluding this chapter, the principal empirical hypotheses stemming from the analysis may be stated briefly.

On the basis of the argument regarding electoral formula, it was suggested that:

1. Under PR, there will be more parties competing per district than under plurality schemes.
2. Under PR, there will be a greater tendency for the same constellation of competing parties to appear in every district than under plurality schemes, and thus there will be fewer different constellations of competing parties in PR systems.
3. Having the same pattern of multiple competitors reproduced in all districts produces a pressure for ideological competition.

On the basis of the argument regarding district magnitude, it was suggested that:

4. More parties will tend to compete in districts returning many members than in districts returning few members.

Taken together, these lead to the first prediction regarding parliamentary party organization:

5. Parties in large district PR systems will be more likely to be ideologically oriented than those competing in plurality systems.

A prediction concerning issue orientation also follows from the argument about district magnitude:

6. Parties competing in small districts will tend to be personalistically oriented or patronage oriented, whereas parties competing in larger districts will tend to be issue oriented.

Although outside the range of a theory about the impact of electoral systems on behavior, it also was suggested that this difference will be greatest when the small districts have more traditional political cultures and the large districts are more modern in orientation.

The nature of interparty choice leads to a prediction regarding the nature of conflict among parties, and particularly regarding the stability of electoral or parliamentary alliances or coalitions:

7. Alliances and coalitions among parties are more likely when there is ordinal choice allowed to the voters than when the voters' choice is categoric.

The nature of choice also leads to a prediction regarding issue orientation:

8. Parties competing in systems with categoric choice will be more issue oriented than parties competing where an ordinal choice is allowed.

Finally, the pattern of cohesion or disunity exhibited by a party in parliament may be predicted from district magnitude, the possibility of intraparty choice, and the distribution of resources in the country:

9. Where there is an intraparty choice, a significant proportion of the parliamentary turnover will result from intraparty competition rather than interparty competition.

10. To the extent that intraparty competition determines a candidate's electoral fortunes, candidates will tend to maintain separate campaign organizations.

11. Externally mobilized resources such as funds or group support are more important in large districts than in small ones.

Hence:

12. Where intraparty choice is allowed, parliamentary parties will tend to be disunited. In the case of small districts, this will be manifested in personalistic fractionalization. In the case of large districts, the pattern of party factionalism or fractionalization will reflect the distribution of electorally mobilizable resources.

It is to the empirical verification of these predictions that attention now must turn.

3

An Extensive Test

ONCE a theory has been developed deductively, it must be tested empirically. In doing this, one may pursue either, or both, of two complementary strategies. On the one hand, the theory may be tested intensively. The greater the number of hypotheses derived from the theory that can be confirmed, the greater will be the confidence that can be placed in the theory. In particular, as the intermediate steps by which a final conclusion is reached are themselves confirmed, confidence is increased in the explanatory power of the theory, as well as in its predictive capacity. On the other hand, a theory may also be tested extensively. The nature and costs of intensive analysis necessarily limit consideration to a small number of cases. While the fit of a variety of data to the predictions of a theory is important in building confidence, so too is the fit of data from a variety of cases taken from the theory's presumed domain. Although fewer, and more general, hypotheses can be tested extensively, the overall validity of the ultimate predictions of a general theory is as important as its detailed fit to a few cases in arguing for its utility. The three chapters following this one are devoted to an intensive test of the theory of electoral systems and party structure just presented, based on data from three European countries. The present chapter reports an extensive test of the theory's general predictions based on data from a random sample of fourteen Western democratic nations.

In constructing a theory one deliberately oversimplifies and abstracts from reality. Simple and clear-cut theoretical concepts replace far more complex realities. Many variables are assumed to be constant when in fact they are not; others are assumed to be irrelevant although in reality they should not be ignored completely. An intensive analysis allows one to make the qualifications and modifications necessary to have the theory fit a particular case. Extensive analysis does not. The fact that the same operational indicator of a theoretical construct may not be the most appropriate for all cases is translated into measurement error. While nonconstant "constants" and ignored variables may average out, in doing so they contribute to unexplained variance. Thus in extensively testing a theory, predictions of fact become hypotheses about tendencies, likelihoods, and proportions. Because of this, and the limited number of cases, the actual hypotheses to be tested differ slightly from those listed at the end of chapter 2. The propositions considered in this chapter are:

1. Parties competing in PR systems will be more likely to be ideological in style than parties competing in plurality systems.
2. Parties competing in small districts will be less issue oriented than parties competing in large districts.
3. Parties competing in systems with ordinal choice will be less issue oriented than parties competing in categoric choice systems.
4. Parties competing in systems with an intraparty choice allowed to voters will be more likely to be factionalized or fractionalized than parties in systems without this kind of choice.

Since these hypotheses involve a number of quite elusive concepts, like ideology, many of which can be measured only indirectly, the observed relationships occasionally may be rather weak. They should, of course, all be in the hypothesized direction.

It is important that one be clear as to what the theory does and does not seek to explain. The theory tries to explain whether or not parties will be ideological in their approaches, not what ideology or combination of specific policy positions any particular party will adopt. It tries to explain whether or not parties will be issue oriented, not which particular issues will be important at any given time. It tries to explain whether or not parties will be cohesive, and if not whether they will be factionalized or fractionalized, not why specific politicians adhere to one or another particular faction.

The indicators of party characteristics employed in this chapter are derived from the data file of the International Comparative Political Parties (ICPP) project. The ICPP data are based on approximately a 50 percent stratified random sample of party systems in existence between 1950 and 1962.[1] The fourteen countries considered here are the modern Western democracies that fell into this sample. Altogether, data concerning forty-nine parties are included, all those winning at least 5 percent of the seats in the lower houses of their national legislatures in at least two successive elections, from 1950 to 1962. Separate coding of variables was done for each of two subperiods, 1950 to 1956 and 1957 to 1962.[2]

One of the problems confronting anyone attempting cross-cultural analysis of political parties is the lack of comparable data. While the professional and journalistic literature describing many parties is enormous, and there is a wealth of information available in official party publications, this material is often in a variety of languages. Furthermore, each work is likely to be based on a separate framework not easily translated to any standardized form usable in a systematic comparative analysis. The ICPP data represent an attempt to overcome this difficulty by deriving from materials available in print, scores on over 100 variables for each party in the sample. The magnitude of this project is illustrated by the total of roughly 20,000 pages indexed for each of the two time periods, just for the forty-nine Anglo-American and Western European parties considered here. The result is a readily accessible summary of our knowledge about each party.

Since this is a rather unusual dataset, a few words about its reliability and validity are required before proceeding with the actual analysis. Notwithstanding the complexity of the task, a quite respectable rate of intercoder reliability (0.79) was achieved through the use of a detailed coding manual providing both theoretical and operational definitions of each variable. As an outside check, the preliminary codes and coders' justifications of them were sent to a large number of area specialists whose evaluations further increased the quality of the data.

The specific variables coded were derived from a conceptual framework that included ten (originally eleven) major aspects of party organization or activity.[3] Against the background of face and content validity established by the reliability of data derived from the coding manual, the construct validity of the variables has been supported by Janda's success in developing scales corresponding to the original concepts and by the high correlation of these scales with independent assessments of the same or similar phenomena.[4] For example, Janda developed a seven-item "Marxism" scale with a reliability of 0.90 from the "issue orientation" cluster of variables. Scores on this scale then were found to correlate highly with both U.S. State Department and Soviet expert ratings of the "right-center-left" orientation of parties.[5]

Since this is a new dataset, and indeed a new type of dataset whose properties are not known fully, findings based on the ICPP data ought to be interpreted both with flexibility and with caution. The ICPP data are especially useful in that they allow parties whose characteristics are not well known to be included without undue effort or expense. Confidence in the overall validity of the coding scheme is increased, however, to the extent that the ICPP coding of well-known cases appears reasonable. Thus, although the analysis in this chapter is primarily statistical in nature, one additional test is made of the validity of the variables used. The scoring of four well-known individual cases, the U.S. Democratic, French Communist, British Conservative, and Irish Fine Gael parties, is cited in each of the tables. Overall, however, this dataset appears to allow analyses at least as reliable as any others based on interpretation of published records and previous research. As always must be the case, it is left to the reader to decide if the variables used in fact indicate what they are claimed to indicate.

The forty-nine parties on which this extensive test of the theory is based are listed in Table 3.1, along with their countries' scores on each of the four dimensions of electoral law suggested to be especially significant. In

TABLE 3.1.
Parties and electoral system characteristics

Country	Parties	Electoral formula		Nature of choice	
		1950–56	1957–62	1950–56	1957–62
United States	Republican Democratic	Plur	Plur	Cat	Cat
United Kingdom	Conservative Labour	Plur	Plur	Cat	Cat
Australia	Labour Liberal Country	Plur	Plur	Ord	Ord
New Zealand	National Labour	Plur	Plur	Cat	Cat
Canada	Progressive-Conservative Liberal New Democratic Social Credit	Plur	Plur	Cat	Cat
Ireland	Fianna Fail Fine Gael Labour	Plur	Plur	Ord	Ord
Austria	People's Socialist Freedom	PR	PR	Cat	Cat
France	Radical MRP Socialist RPF/UNR Communist	PR	Plur	Cat	Cat
W. Germany	Christian Democratic Socialist Free Democratic	PR	PR	Cat	Cat
Denmark	Social Democratic Venstre Conservative Radikale	PR	PR	Cat	Cat
Iceland	Independence Progressive People's Union Social Democratic	PR	PR	Cat	Cat
Sweden	Social Democratic Center Liberal Conservative	PR	PR	Cat	Cat
Netherlands	Catholic People's Labor Liberal Antirevolutionary Christian Historical Union Communist	PR	PR	Cat	Cat
Luxembourg	Christian Social Socialist Labour Democratic Communist	PR	PR	Ord	Ord

* These figures are averages computed over all elections in the relevant subperiod.
† Rae apparently counts the four regional districts used for the distribution of remainders as additi
districts, for a total of twenty-nine. Douglas Rae, *The Political Consequences of Electoral Laws* (
Haven: Yale University Press, 1971), p. 42.

Number of districts*		Number of deputies*		Size of electorate* (10,000s)		Preference voting	
1950–56	1957–62	1950–56	1957–62	1950–56	1957–62	1950–56	1957–62
435	435	435	435	10,222	10,967	Eff	Eff
627	630	627	630	3,487	3,540	None	None
123	124	123	124	483	555	None	None
80	80	80	80	121	127	None	None
265	265	265	265	840	924	None	None
40	38	147	146	177	170	Eff	Eff
25†	25†	165	165	463	475	Ineff	Ineff
82	465	544	465	2,565	2,739	Ineff	None
10‡	10‡	487	498	3,320	3,642	None	None
23	23	158	175	259	281	Eff§	Eff§
28	8	52	56	9	10	Eff	Eff
28	28	230	231	485	498	Ineff	Ineff
1	1	125	150	596	659	Ineff	Ineff
4	4	52	52	18	18	Eff	Eff

This is the number of lander districts. About half the members of the Bundestag are elected from gle-member districts, the other half from the lander lists based on national PR.
The Danish Social Democratic party was coded as having Ineffective preference voting.

accordance with the discussion in chapter 2, the Irish system of multi-member constituencies with a single transferable ballot has been coded as a plurality system, although it usually is referred to as a PR system. The fact that it is oriented toward candidates and order, rather than toward parties and vote shares, outweighs the reasonably high proportionality of the results.

The only other electoral system descriptor requiring elaboration is the intraparty preference vote. While this variable is simple conceptually, some electoral systems have been devised that make it less clear-cut empirically. In many countries where a preference vote is allowed formally, far less than a majority of the voters actually avail themselves of this opportunity. If the order in which candidates are elected is determined solely by the explicitly cast preference votes, this causes no ambiguity. In other cases, however, the parties may be allowed, by one device or another, effectively to cast the preference votes of those of their supporters not explicitly voting otherwise. One possibility is for their votes to be counted as votes for the party list in the order presented by the party. For example, in the Netherlands, unless an individual candidate obtains one-half of the list quotient in his district, all votes are awarded to the first candidate on the party list up to the number needed for election, the remainder going to the second candidate on the list until he is elected, and so forth, with the effect that the party, not the voters (except by passive acquiescence), actually determines who is elected.[6] A second possibility is available to parties in Denmark, where a ballot cast without an explicitly marked preference vote may be counted as a preference vote for the party's nominee in that voter's election district within the larger PR constituency. By nominating its preferred candidates in districts where it is strong, the party instead of the voters again can decide who will be elected.[7] Still another possibility, which was employed at times in France, is for the list order submitted by the party to prevail unless it is explicitly changed by at least 50 percent of the party's voters. Given the generally low salience of preferential voting, this never occurred in France.[8] In Table 3.1, countries are listed as having an effective, an ineffective, or no intraparty preference vote (none) according to whether this facility is available at all and, if so, whether or not it regularly influences the outcome of elections.

Electoral Formula and Ideology

The first general hypothesis to be tested concerns the relationship between electoral formula and the degree to which parties behave ideologically. Because PR rewards all transfers of votes equally, regardless of source or destination, and because it encourages parties to compete even in areas where they are weak, PR makes it likely that each party will face the same competitive situation in every district. Further, under PR the party usually will be forced to defend its "policy territory" against encroachment from more than one direction at a time, thus creating pressure to adopt a "point" rather than a "tendency" as the party platform. It is in rationalizing the peculiar virtues of the particular point chosen and in creating linkages among otherwise independent issue and policy questions that an ideology is especially useful. Thus the prediction was made that parties competing under PR systems would be more likely to be ideological in style than would those in plurality systems.[9]

Ideological behavior, as distinct from adherence to a particular ideology, has proven extraordinarily difficult to measure empirically. The ICPP data allow measures of three different aspects or manifestations of ideological style to be constructed. The first is based on the extremism or moderation of individual policy positions taken, and reflects one notion of ideology implicit in the "end of ideology" literature.[10] The second is concerned with the consistency of party positions across issues, and taps the notion of "constraint" typical of research concerning the ideological sophistication of mass publics.[11] Finally, the third addresses the question of whether the party professes adherence to some general doctrine, and relates directly to the notion of ideological style developed in chapter 2. Because of the small number of cases involved, and the obvious crudity of some of the operational measures, each indicator will be presented as a dichotomy. Alone, none is an adequate indicator of the nature of a party's ideological style. Rather, each refers to patterns of behavior that may be expected to vary with, or result from, ideological behavior.

To say that a party is ideological in approach is to suggest that the positions it takes on individual issues are derived from adherence to a general underlying philosophy of government or society. It is not necessary that the issue position adopted be either unpopular or extreme. Although steadfast support of an unpopular position may be some indication of ideological commitment, a party might equally espouse the dominant ideology in its country and consequently enjoy continuous electoral success.[12] Nonetheless, ideology appears to play an important role in democratic politics only when there is significant ideological disagreement—something unlikely to occur in plurality systems with their tendencies to produce policy convergence. Although the American Democratic and Republican parties each might emphasize ideological concerns if they were in competition with European socialist or religious parties, they do not do so when competing only with each other. Because both American parties espouse the same ideology, the conflict between them tends to be pragmatic. Thus, while a centrist or moderate ideology is entirely possible, one would expect to find it overtly manifested only in apposition to more extreme positions. Extremism is not a necessary condition for ideology, but it is likely to be a sufficient one. Accordingly, the first operational indicator of ideological style to be considered is taking extreme policy positions.

The policy orientations of parties in the ICPP data were scored on each of thirteen issues covering a wide range of domestic and foreign policy questions. These issues were:

1. ownership of the means of production;
2. economic planning;
3. distribution of wealth;
4. providing for social welfare;
5. secularization of society;
6. allocation of resources to armed services;
7. alignment with East/West blocs;
8. anticolonialism;
9. supranational integration;
10. national integration;
11. popular participation;
12. protection of civil rights;
13. interference with civil liberties.

For each issue, an eleven-point scale was constructed to reflect both the rhetoric and the activities of the party in question. These scales run between +5 (PRO-strong) and −5 (ANTI-strong), with 0 reserved for ambiguous or contradictory positions. For example, a +5 on the ownership of the means of production scale represented:

strongly favors government ownership; advocates government ownership of all basic industries; advocates ownership of means of production generally.

A score of −5 was:

strongly opposes government ownership; opposes even government regulation of production and marketing activities of industries other than minimal requirements for health, safety, and honesty; urges repeal of present regulations.

On the secularization of society scale, a +5 was equivalent to:

advocates expropriation of church property and/or official discouragement of religious practice.

A score of −5 was equivalent to:

advocates establishment of a state religion; imposition of a system of laws based on religious prescription.

Ratings for the other issues were defined similarly. If no information could be found for a party, it was coded as "missing" rather than 0; parties were scored even if all parties within the country adhered to the same consensual position on that issue so that it was electorally irrelevant within that system. Coming in equally from each end of the scales, and dichotomizing each scale as nearly as possible between the most extreme (and thus presumptively ideological) one-fourth and the more moderate three-fourths of the parties, the hypothesis is that parties competing under PR will be more likely to adopt extreme positions than will parties competing in plurality systems.

In testing this hypothesis, only eleven of these variables were considered. Issue 7, alignment with East/West blocs, was deleted as being inappropriate to parties the vast majority of which *are* the Western bloc (so that extreme pro-Western orientation is more tautological than illuminating). Issue 10, national integration, was eliminated because inspection of the data suggested it was excessively determined by idiosyncratic historical factors. Further, it was the only issue on which the notoriously ideological French Communist party was coded as having a moderate position while the clearly nonideological Australian Country party had an extreme position. These findings raised serious doubts as to the validity of this particular issue variable as an indicator of ideological style.

Table 3.2 reports the distributions of extreme and nonextreme positions taken by parties competing under the two electoral formulae for each of the eleven remaining issues. For each relationship, the value and statistical significance of Kendall's tau-b is reported first, and then the value of Goodman and Kruskal's gamma.[13] As these tables are constructed, the correlation coefficients all are expected to be positive.

The data in the table reveal regular and significant support for the hypothesis, especially in the first subperiod. Twenty of the twenty-two correlations are in the expected direction, seventeen significantly so as a level of $p < 0.10$. (This unusually weak significance level was chosen because of the small number of cases and the crudity of measurement.) Neither of the two negative correlations observed differed significantly from 0, even at this low level.

The extremism of a party's position on any particular issue may be affected by a variety of historical or situational factors in addition, or in opposition, to its general ideological tendency. When averaged over a number of issues, however, these confounding influences will be of considerably reduced importance. For this reason, a summary measure of ideological tendency based on extremism was computed by counting the number of issues out of the eleven on which each party took an extreme position. When dichotomized at three or more versus two or fewer a quite strong tau of 0.514 was observed for the first subperiod, and a strong tau of 0.414 was observed for the second subperiod, both significant at better than $p < 0.005$. (See Table 3.3, number of extreme positions.)

Overall, it appears that parties competing in countries with PR are more likely than other parties to adopt extreme policy positions, and hence are inferred to be more ideological in style. If, as suggested, this has the

TABLE 3.2.
Ideology as indicated by issue extremism on individual issues versus electoral formula

Issue	Position*	1950–56 Formula PR	Plur.	Tau-b	Sig.	Gamma	1957–1962 Formula PR	Plur.	Tau-b	Sig.	Gamma
Ownership of means of production	Extreme[d] Moderate[abc]	12 21	1 15	0.320	0.02	0.791	8 20	2 19	0.234	0.06	0.583
Economic planning	Extreme[d] Moderate[abc]	9 23	1 15	0.254	0.05	0.709	6 21	3 18	0.101	NS	0.263
Distribution of wealth	Extreme[d] Moderate[abc]	12 17	3 12	0.214	0.09	0.477	9 15	5 15	0.134	NS	0.286
Providing for social welfare	Extreme[d] Moderate[abc]	11 22	6 10	0.041	NS	0.091	9 19	8 13	−0.062	NS	−0.130
Secularization of society	Extreme[d] Moderate[abc]	22 10	3 12	0.455	0.001	0.796	17 10	7 13	0.277	0.04	0.519
Alloc. of resources to armed services	Extreme[a] Moderate[bd]	11 19	2 13	0.243	0.06	0.580	9 16	3 17	0.236	0.06	0.522
Anticolonialism	Extreme[b1cd] Moderate[ab2]	15 14	4 11	0.240	0.06	0.493	5 19	7 13	−0.158	NS	−0.343
Supranational integration	Extreme[cd] Moderate[ab]	18 11	5 11	0.295	0.03	0.565	15 9	8 13	0.244	0.06	0.461
Popular participation	Extreme[bcd] Moderate[a]	30 0	10 5	0.500	0.001	1.000	25 0	15 5	0.395	0.005	1.000
Protection of civil rights	Extreme[d] Moderate[ab]	10 9	3 12	0.333	0.03	0.632	8 6	5 15	0.326	0.04	0.600
Interference with civil liberties	Extreme Moderate[ab]	6 26	0 14	0.256	0.05	1.000	6 22	0 18	0.311	0.02	1.000

* Superscripts identify the coding of the U.S. Democrats (a), British Conservatives (b), Irish Fine Gael (c), and French Communists (d). When a party was coded differently for the two time periods, the letter code is tagged with 1 (1950–56) and 2 (1957–62). If a letter is omitted, the corresponding party was coded as missing data for that variable.

44

additional effect of making ideological behavior by moderate parties more likely, Tables 3.2 and 3.3 may even understate the relationship between electoral formula and ideology. With these measures, however, it is impossible to tell.

A second indicator of ideology is consistency. Since ideological parties derive their specific policy positions from an underlying philosophy, it is more likely that the positions they take on different specific issues related to the same basic dimension will be consistent with one another than would be positions taken by a party interested only in vote mongering.[14] In Converse's terms, the policy positions of ideologically oriented parties should exhibit "constraint."[15] The problem is that consistency is a subjective concept, and hence this definition of ideology is more suitable for testing adherence to some particular ideology defined on a priori grounds than for testing for the presence of ideology in general. Who, for example, is to say that the positions Converse defines as being "liberal" on civil rights and foreign policy really "ought" to go together?

Within the confines of Western culture, however, some issues may be assumed to go together in any reasonable ideology. Among the ICPP variables, the questions of economic planning and ownership of the means of production are two such issues. Each taps an aspect of the left-right dimension that is pervasive in Western politics. These two issues were among the most highly correlated with Janda's Marxism scale for the whole 158-party dataset, and are the most highly correlated pair of variables within the 49-party subset considered here. Without specifying the relationship of this dimension to other dimensions of public policy, that is, without specifying any particular ideology, it remains reasonable to expect that ideological parties will be more likely to take consistent positions on these two issues than will their nonideological counterparts. Taking identical or adjacent scores on the eleven-point issue scales as the measure of consistency (ideological behavior), the expectation is that parties competing in PR systems will be disproportionately consistent.

As the data for policy consistency in Table 3.3 show, this is the case for these forty-nine parties. Even in the second subperiod, when the relationship is weaker, parties in PR systems are about 15 percent more likely to have consistent positions than are parties in plurality systems. While the resulting tau-b of 0.154 is not significant at the 0.10 level, the corresponding tau-b for the first subperiod, for which the difference in likelihood of having consistent positions is over 25 percent, was 0.241, significant at the level of $p < 0.06$. It is important to note that this relationship is not just a function of the relative extremism of parties in PR systems. In fact, the relationship holds more strongly for parties with moderate positions than for those at the extremes. In this respect too, ideological behavior is more common among parties in PR systems.

TABLE 3.3.
Ideology as indicated by number of extreme issue positions taken, policy consistency, and doctrinism versus electoral formula

	1950–56				1957–62			
	Formula	Tau-b	Sig.	Gamma	Formula	Tau-b	Sig.	Gamma
	PR Plur.				PR Plur.			
Number of extreme* positions								
Three or more[cd]	30 7	0.514	0.001	0.856	25 11	0.414	0.002	0.767
Two or fewer[ab]	3 9				3 10			
Policy consistency*								
Consistent[d]	22 7	0.241	0.05	0.478	17 10	0.154	NS	0.303
Inconsistent[abc]	10 9				10 11			
Doctrinism*								
High[d]	24 4	0.452	0.001	0.778	21 7	0.417	0.002	0.714
Low[abc]	9 12				7 14			

* Superscripts identify the coding of the U.S. Democrats (a), British Conservatives (b), Irish Fine Gael (c), and French Communists (d).

The final manifestation of ideology comes perhaps closest to the definition implicit in chapter 2. It concerns the degree to which a party has a specific and identifiable body of general philosophy or doctrine to which it can point as the source of authority for its goals, policies, and other actions. This aspect of ideology relates directly to the distinction between pragmatic, vote mongering, parties and parties of principle. The former choose positions solely on the basis of electoral advantage and idiosyncratic factors with no pretense of logical consistency. Parties of principle, in contrast, insist on ideological purity even at the cost of electoral advantage.[16] Consistency, again, is definable only in subjective terms. One might judge a party highly consistent even in the absence of an explicit general doctrine or one might judge a party inconsistent even though it had such a statement of principles. Nevertheless, the existence of a written body of party principles to which constant references are made is certainly indicative of an ideological style.

The ICPP data include a variable that measures the degree of doctrinism of each party in these terms. This variable provides strong support for the hypothesized correlation between PR and ideological style, when the variable is dichotomized between parties for which "There is a body of literature that can be said to embody party doctrine, and members refer to it continually," and parties without such a written doctrine, and cross-tabulated against electoral formula. For the second subperiod, the observed value of tau-b is 0.417, strong enough to be significant at the 0.002 level, even with only forty-nine cases. For the first subperiod, the relationship is even stronger, with tau-b equal to 0.452 (significant at $p < 0.001$). Naturally, the gamma coefficients are even higher, 0.714 for the second subperiod and 0.778 for the first. (See Table 3.3, doctrinism).

Overall then, there is considerable support for the hypothesis that electoral formula affects the level of ideological concern among political parties. Although some of the observed correlations were not terribly strong, many were. For each of three separate indicators of ideological style the forty-nine parties considered here provide evidence of a higher incidence of ideology among parties competing under PR systems than among those in plurality systems.

Finally, before leaving the relationship between ideology and electoral formula, it should be observed that these data also support two of the intermediate predictions that led to the expectation that parties in PR systems would be more likely to be ideological in style. First, the number of significant parties competing is greater in PR systems. Although the original argument, and the intensive test in chapter 4, actually refer to the number of parties competing at the district level, it still is instructive to note that the number of parties that meet the criteria for inclusion in the ICPP dataset was on average lower for the plurality systems than for those with PR.

Second, there is some direct evidence for the convergence of issue positions taken by parties in plurality systems. As already shown, parties in such systems are individually more likely to take moderate positions. In addition, at the national level, the standard deviation of the positions taken by parties on each issue also tends to be lower for the plurality systems (even after correction for the number of cases).

District Magnitude and Issue Orientation

The second general hypothesis that was advanced related the size of parliamentary districts to the degree of policy concern displayed by the parties competing within them. In constituencies with large populations, candidates are unlikely to be able to provide personalistic services to enough voters to compete successfully on this basis. Likewise, the effectiveness of appeals based on local ties or individual acquaintance or loyalty is limited by the number of friends one individual can have. Consequently, it was suggested that parties competing in large districts would be more likely to stress policy concerns in their campaigns, and thus would be more policy oriented in general, than parties competing in smaller districts. Since personalistic and localistic ties are especially characteristic of traditional societies, it was suggested further that this tendency would be especially pronounced when the small districts were less advanced culturally and economically.

To test this hypothesis, each electoral system was coded according to the average size of its electorate per district and per deputy. Population per district then was dichotomized at 60,000 and population per deputy at 20,000 eligible voters. Traditional orientation was indicated indirectly by percentage nonurban in the population, dichotomized at 60 percent; percentage of the economically active population employed in agriculture, dichotomized at 20 percent; and radio receivers per 1,000 population, dichotomized at 300.

Three manifestations of issue orientation were considered. The first was based on the clarity with which the party's individual issue positions could be discerned. The second concerns the level of debate within the party over matters of policy and philosophy. Finally, the third measures the degree to which party militants are motivated by policy concerns rather than by material benefits, personalism, or the simple desire to win elections for its own sake.

Along with the policy positions taken by parties over the range of issues already discussed, the ICPP data include for each variable an "adequacy-confidence" score based on the availability and consistency of the evidence considered. Emphasis on issue positions should lead to clear articulation of party policy stands, and this in turn should lead to the ready availability of consistent information in the professional and journalistic literature concerning those stands. For this reason, the adequacy-confidence scores for the eleven specific issues considered were used to indicate policy orientation. These were dichotomized between the category labeled "Adequate: low to medium," implying either that no source had complete information regarding the party's position on that issue or else that there was significant disagreement among sources consulted, and the category labeled "Adequate: medium," which required one uncontested source giving adequate data for a coding to be made.

Examination of the cross-tabulations of the two measures of district magnitude against the dichotomized adequacy-confidence scores (not reproduced here) shows at best weak support for the hypothesis. For the measure of population per district, only nine of the twenty-two correlations observed were significantly different from 0, and of these, only seven were positive (as expected). Similarly, only seven of the correlations between the measure of population per deputy and the adequacy-confidence scores were significantly different from 0, six of them being positive.

As was done for the relationship between electoral formula and ideology as indicated by issue extremism, a summary measure was computed by collapsing the eleven individual scores and dichotomizing between parties with vague issue positions on at least six issues on the one hand and those with vague positions on no more than five on the other. Cross-tabulating this summary measure against the two district magnitude variables yields a moderate correlation in the expected direction for both subperiods, all statistically significant at the level of $p < 0.08$ or better (Table 3.4).

The second set of indicators of issue orientation is based on the level of internal policy debate within the party. These variables were constructed from the measures of "issue factionalism" and "ideological factionalism" coded in the ICPP data. The issue factionalism variable was concerned with disputes over discrete policy questions, while the ideological factionalism variable was based on conflicts over more general orientations. For example, the split between northern and southern Democrats in the United States would represent ideological factionalism while division between hawks and doves over the Vietnam war would be issue factionalism. While these measures were concerned primarily with the size and organization of opposing groups within the party, they can be dichotomized between parties in which issues are "subject to public debate and disagreement among party leaders" and those in which they are not. In this form, each may be taken as evidence of concern over issues, with the expectation that when some matter is of importance to a party, there will be noticeable internal debate concerning it.

When these variables are cross-tabulated against the district magnitude measures, the result indicates very weak support for the hypothesized correlation with population per district, but quite strong support with

TABLE 3.4.
Issue orientation as indicated by number of low clarity issue positions versus district magnitude

District magnitude	Number of low clarity positions*		Tau-b	Sig.	Gamma
	Six or more	Five or fewer[abcd]			
1950–56					
Population <60,000	6	16	0.208	0.08	0.500
Population >60,000	3	24			
1957–62					
Population <60,000	7	20	0.216	0.07	0.556
Population >60,000	2	20			
1950–56					
Population per deputy <20,000	5	12	0.208	0.08	0.489
Population per deputy >20,000	4	28			
1957–62					
Population per deputy <20,000	5	12	0.208	0.08	0.489
Population per deputy >20,000	4	28			

* Superscripts identify the coding of the U.S. Democrats (a), British Conservatives (b), Irish Fine Gael (c), and French Communists (d).

respect to population per deputy. As Table 3.5 shows, in the former case only one of four values of tau-b was significantly different from 0, and that was still less than 0.20. For the population per deputy tabulations, however, all four correlations were over 0.30, the weakest one being significant at the level of $p < 0.02$. Apparently, the size of each deputy's share of the electorate is more important in determining a party's issue orientation than is the electorate's total size.

For the final indicator of issue orientation, the importance of purposive incentives, however, the relative importance of district population and population per deputy is reversed. Although all four values of tau-b shown in Table 3.6 are positive as expected, only one is significantly different from 0 and that was for the relationship between purposive incentives and population per district.

Correlating the issue orientation variables with the indicators of a traditional social system revealed no strong direct relationships. Only four of the twelve correlations were significantly different from 0, those between the measures of issue and ideological debate and the level of agricultural employment, and those between ideological debate and purposive incentives and the penetration of radio. In all four cases, a more traditional social system was associated with lower levels of issue orientation. Returning to the original relationship between district magnitude and issue orientation and controlling for each of the indicators of traditionalism shows the impact of district size to be generally greater in more traditional countries and less in more modern ones. To test more directly the suggestion that the effects of

TABLE 3.5.
Issue orientation as indicated by issue and ideological debate versus district magnitude

District magnitude	Issue debate*					Ideological debate*				
	No[cd]	Yes[ab]	Tau-b	Sig.	Gamma	No[cd]	Yes[ab]	Tau-b	Sig.	Gamma
1950–56										
Population <60,000	6	15	0.110	NS	0.253	7	15	0.154	NS	0.345
Population >60,000	5	21				5	22			
1957–62										
Population <60,000	6	20	−0.009	NS	−0.020	8	19	0.191	0.10	0.455
Population >60,000	5	16				3	19			
1950–56										
Population per deputy <20,000	7	10	0.316	0.02	0.640	8	9	0.383	0.005	0.723
Population per deputy >20,000	4	26				4	28			
1957–62										
Population per deputy <20,000	8	9	0.421	0.05	0.778	8	9	0.429	0.002	0.792
Population per deputy >20,000	3	27				3	29			

* Superscripts identify the coding of the U.S. Democrats (a), British Conservatives (b), Irish Fine Gael (c), and French Communists (d).

TABLE 3.6.

Issue orientation as indicated by the importance of purposive incentives versus district magnitude

District magnitude	Purposive incentives*		Tau-b	Sig.	Gamma
	Unimportant[ac]	Important[bd]			
1950–56					
Population <60,000	11	7	0.262	0.05	0.496
Population >60,000	9	17			
1957–62					
Population <60,000	12	10	0.165	NS	0.322
Population >60,000	8	13			
1950–56					
Population per deputy <20,000	7	6	0.109	NS	0.235
Population per deputy >20,000	13	18			
1957–62					
Population per deputy <20,000	8	6	0.089	NS	0.208
Population per deputy >20,000	16	17			

* Superscripts identify the coding of the U.S. Democrats (a), British Conservatives (b), Irish Fine Gael (c), and French Communists (d).

traditionalism and magnitude would be additive, a series of cross-tabulations was made using only small traditional and large modern district systems. These tables showed substantially increased correlations in most cases.

Although there is no substantial evidence to suggest that the proposed relationship between district magnitude and issue orientation is incorrect, it must be admitted that the supporting evidence is fairly weak. While all but one of the correlations with the summary measures of issue orientation were in the expected direction, only for the relationships between the indicators of internal policy debate and population per deputy could they be called reasonably strong. Future research must determine whether this is because the relationship is overwhelmed by other forces, because the threshold of "smallness" was set too high,[17] or because the relationship is, in fact, either trivial or incorrectly specified.[18] At the present, however, one safely can reject the null hypothesis of no relationship, but one must have doubts about the strength of the relationship that exists.

Nature of Choice and
Issue Orientation

It also was suggested that when voters are allowed to split the weight of their ballots among parties or to specify the transfer of their votes from a candidate of one party to a candidate of another, parties and their candidates will tend to emphasize characteristics like personality and locality that allow effective appeals across party lines while minimizing the apparent sharpness of the issue differences between them. In terms of the measures used in the preceding section, this hypothesis leads to the expectation that parties competing in systems with ordinal choice will be less issue oriented than those competing where a categoric choice is forced on the voters.

As was the case with district magnitude, only weak support for this hypothesis could be shown by examining the cross-tabulations of the clarity and consistency with which individual issue positions could be discerned by the ICPP coders against the nature of choice (again not shown). While seventeen of the twenty-two correlations were positive, only seven were statistically significant. (None of the negative correlations were significant.) Nonetheless, a simple binomial test against the null hypothesis that positive and negative signs are equally likely shows this pattern to be significant at the level of $p < 0.01$. Thus, one can conclude that there is a relationship between issue orientation, as indicated by the adequacy-confidence scores, and the nature of choice.

This conclusion is reinforced by the data in Table 3.7, based on the dichotomized summary measure. Here the relationship between party orientation and electoral system was perceptibly stronger than for district magnitude, with the tau-b for each subperiod equal to 0.283, significant at the level of $p < 0.03$.

Evidence based on the indicators of issue and ideological debate and of the importance of purposive incentives in motivating activists shows even stronger support for the hypothesis. These data all are reported in Table 3.8. Correlations over 0.30 were found between the nature of choice and both issue and ideological debate within the parties. Only slightly weaker correlations were observed for the prevalance of purposive incentives as factors motivating party militants. All six of these correlations were statistically significant at the level of $p < 0.03$ or better.

Summarizing these findings, then, there is significant evidence that the degree to which parties are issue oriented is affected by the formal characteristics of the electoral system in which they compete. This effect is strongest with regard to the nature of choice allowed to the voters, but district magnitude clearly plays a role as well.[19]

Intraparty Choice and Party Unity

The final hypothesis to be tested with the ICPP data concerns the relationship between an intraparty preference vote and the degree to which the party will be cohesive. When voters are allowed no free choice among a party's candidates, competition, especially in the electoral arena, naturally is focused between or among parties. Depending on how preference voting

TABLE 3.7.
Issue orientation as indicated by number of low clarity positions versus nature of choice

Number of low clarity positions*	1950–56					1957–62				
	Nature of choice		Tau-b	Sig.	Gamma	Nature of choice		Tau-b	Sig.	Gamma
	Ord.	Cat.				Ord.	Cat.			
Six or more	4	5	0.283	0.03	0.639	4	5	0.283	0.03	0.639
Five or fewer[abcd]	6	34				6	34			

* Superscripts identify the coding of the U.S. Democrats (a), British Conservatives (b), Irish Fine Gael (c), and French Communists (d).

is structured, its existence creates either the opportunity or the necessity for intraparty electoral competition. Such competition should operate as a powerful discourager of intraparty unity in all spheres. The necessity of competing against other members of their own party for reelection tends to force deputies to develop independent electoral bases and independent access to the resources necessary for campaigning. Simultaneously, this independence denies the party organization an important hold over its representatives and makes deputies sensitive to the demands of individuals or groups other than the party. Where resources are diffused throughout the country, each candidate can build an independent personal organization based on autonomous access to supporters backing only him. This independence of candidates will allow, and indeed encourage, individual independence among the elected, and thus a fractionalized party. Where control over resources is concentrated in a few hands, however, organized factions are likely to appear, cemented by the fact that each faction's members are dependent on the same sponsors. In either event, however, the expectation is that parties competing where a preference vote is allowed will be less cohesive than others.

Two indicators of party factionalism or fractionalization can be constructed from variables included in the ICPP data. As already mentioned, measures of issue and ideological factionalism were coded for each party. Along with these, measures of strategic and leadership factionalism also were included. Since the hypothesis suggests factionalism without specifying the particular form it might take, these four variables were combined into one. That variable then was dichotomized between parties with either large or small factions having at least some formal organization and all others. Thus, the level of organization of the competing factions, rather than the simple existence of open debate, was used as the measure of factionalism.[20]

The second indicator was constructed from the "leadership concentration" variable. The natural effect of fractionalization or factionalism within a party is to limit the possibility that one leader will be able to assume unquestioned command.[21] Conversely, the number of individuals claiming a share in leadership of the party should increase. The nature of the party

TABLE 3.8.
Issue orientation as indicated by issue and ideological debate and the importance of purposive incentives versus nature of choice

Issue orientation[*]	1950–56 Nature of choice					1957–62 Nature of choice				
	Ord.	Cat.	Tau-b	Sig.	Gamma	Ord.	Cat.	Tau-b	Sig.	Gamma
Issue debate										
No[cd]	5	6	0.327	0.02	0.676	5	6	0.327	0.02	0.676
Yes[ab]	5	31				5	31			
Ideological debate										
No[cd]	5	7	0.300	0.02	0.641	5	6	0.334	0.02	0.692
Yes[ab]	5	32				5	33			
Purposive incentives										
Unimportant[ac]	5	15	0.302	0.03	0.769	5	15	0.297	0.03	0.760
Important[bd]	1	23				1	22			

[*] Superscripts identify the coding of the U.S. Democrats (a), British Conservatives (b), Irish Fine Gael (c), and French Communists (d).

constitution, the intensity of cleavages among the competing leaders, the leaders' willingness to compromise, and the competitive situation of the party as a whole all may contribute to the determination of whether these individuals cooperatively control the party or continue to vie openly with one another so as to prevent collective centralization. In any case, the expectation is that where there is a preference vote, the number of first-rank leaders of each party will be large. Accordingly, the leadership concentration variable was dichotomized between the categories:

Leadership is clearly decentralized: there are more than five leaders who frequently make pronouncements in behalf of the national party, but they are not regarded authoritatively binding spokesmen

and

Leadership is collectively centralized into a group of more than five party leaders: decisions of this group are regarded as authoritatively binding on the party; there may be a party leader, but he along (sic) is not powerful enough to control party policy

on the one hand, and all other categories on the other.

No relationship of any consequence is shown when one compares effective preference voting and the measure constructed from the factionalism variables. As the results for effective preference voting in Table 3.9 show, the observed sign of tau-b is negative (the expectation was that it would be positive), but only in the first subperiod is it more than trivially different from 0.

This unexpected result is brought about jointly by a surplus of apparently factionalized parties in systems without preference voting and of nonfac-tionalized parties where preference voting exists. A number of explanations

TABLE 3.9.
Factionalism versus preference voting

	Factionalism*				
	Yes[a2]	No[a1bcd]	Tau-b	Sig.	Gamma
Effective preference voting					
1950–56					
Yes	2	14	−0.194	0.09	−0.505
No	10	23			
1957–62					
Yes	4	12	−0.024	NS	−0.059
No	9	24			
Any preference voting					
1950–56					
Yes	8	27	−0.060	NS	−0.149
No	4	10			
1957–62					
Yes	10	25	0.073	NS	0.189
No	3	11			

* Superscripts identify the coding of the U.S. Democrats (a), British Conservatives (b), Irish Fine Gael (c), and French Communists (d). When a party was coded differently for the two time periods, the letter code is tagged with 1 (1950–56) and 2 (1957–62).

for this result present themselves and require further analysis. The first concerns the coding of the preferential vote variable. As already explained, only countries in which the preference vote regularly plays a role in determining electoral outcomes were coded as having effective preferential voting. This variable thus combines two phenomena, one legal/structural and the other behavioral. But perhaps the regular importance of preferential voting is less significant than its *potential* importance. The logic here would be that factions or individuals who are dissatisfied with their relative standing within the party could appeal over the heads of party councils directly to the voters. As a result, those councils are led to find compromises that make overt conflict unnecessary. In this case, the mere existence of preference voting would pose a credible threat that might be used to advantage by candidates. Under these circumstances, the possibility of intraparty conflict would replace the direct requirements of intraparty campaigning as the incentive to factionalism. Recoding the preference variable to reflect this possibility (recoding the parties from Sweden, Austria, the Netherlands, France, and the Danish Social Democrats) yields the results shown for any preference voting versus no preference voting in Table 3.9. Note that the correlations are still low, but at least one has become positive.

The existence of a preference vote not only encourages factions to form, but also makes their survival within a party easier. This fact is illustrated by the parties in systems with no preferential voting that nonetheless were factionalized. As Table 3.9 shows, there were four such parties in the first subperiod and three in the second among the forty-nine parties analyzed here. Of these, two experienced splits during the time for which data were collected by the ICPP project, while only one of the ten factionalized parties in systems having at least a formal preference vote split during this period.

A second possibility is that none of the bases of factionalism included in the construction of the composite index was of sufficient salience for a party for factions to emerge, even given favorable conditions. These then would have been coded as nonfactionalized, even though factions might exist based on other cleavages. While this seems unlikely given the range of possible bases considered, the complementary possibility that a party might appear united on a dimension as a result of nearly total disinterest in it must be taken more seriously. A real test of this proposition is beyond the power of the data available. Some indication of its possible value can be gained by regarding as cases of "missing data" rather than as united parties those parties for which none of the four questions was a matter for public disagreement and debate among leaders. Doing this yields weak positive correlations whichever way preference voting is dichotomized.

Finally, two additional considerations must be raised. First, the hypothesis is that preference voting will lead to disunity, of which factionalism is only one of two possible manifestations. With this measure of factionalism, there is no way to identify parties that are simply disunited, although the fact that the American Republican party is coded as "united" illustrates the seriousness of this problem. Second, the conditions (suggested in chapter 2) under which factions would be the expected manifestation of disunity—conditions not met by the Republicans—cannot be tested with this dataset. Cross-tabulations in which the locus of control over nominations and control of party mass media are held constant suggest that concentration of control increases the likelihood that factions will emerge; presumably diffusion of control would lead to fractionalization. Yet there is no way to tell whether this is a result of the truth of the hypothesis or the vagaries of data availability. Treatment of these problems must await the intensive analysis to follow.

The hypothesis that party unity behind a single leader or small group of leaders is discouraged by preference voting clearly is confirmed by the indicator based on leadership concentration. Parties competing in systems without effective preference voting were found to be about equally likely to have many or few leaders, while those where there is effective intraparty voting were more than three times as likely to have leadership diffused among many, rather than few, individuals. When the preference voting variable is recoded to combine all parties from systems with preference voting, whether regularly effective or not, the strength of the relationship is doubled for the second subperiod, but surprisingly reduced by about 25 percent for the first subperiod. (See Table 3.10.)

TABLE 3.10.
Number of party leaders versus preference voting

| | Number of party leaders* | | | | |
	Five or more[a]	Four or fewer[b][d]	Tau-b	Sig.	Gamma
Effective preference voting					
1950–56					
Yes	10	3	0.258	0.05	0.560
No	16	17			
1957–62					
Yes	10	3	0.180	NS	0.421
No	19	14			
Any preference voting					
1950–56					
Yes	20	12	0.182	NS	0.379
No	6	8			
1957–62					
Yes	24	8	0.375	0.01	0.688
No	5	9			

* Superscripts identify the coding of the U.S. Democrats (a), British Conservatives (b), Irish Fine Gael (c), and French Communists (d). If a letter is omitted, the corresponding party was coded as missing data for that variable.

Considering both measures, there is some evidence that preferential voting and party disunity are associated, although the case is certainly stronger for the diffusion of leadership measure. Before leaving this point, however, one final complication must be raised. The existence of preferential voting appears to be strongly correlated with the nationalization of formal party structure. Where preferential voting is allowed, functions such as dispersal of funds, selection of candidates, and formulation of policy tend to be performed by national boards instead of by a single national leader, but also instead of by local or regional councils or conventions. The most likely explanation for this administrative shift is that it aids in maintaining party stability by furthering compromise. Any particular faction may be dominant locally and both willing and able to ignore the interests and desires of others. At the national level, however, leaders with a primary stake in protecting the party from open splits are more likely to reach compromise solutions, perhaps based on some form of proportionality.[22] A possible consequence of this willingness to compromise might be that open factionalism is suppressed, thus weakening the observed relationship between preferential voting and the factionalism measure. Nonetheless, the diffusion of leadership measure remains sensitive to this kind of situation.

In summary, the data analyzed here offer limited but important support to the deductive theory. Ignoring the indicators of factionalism, which clearly were the most questionable in terms of both validity and appropriateness to the hypotheses tested, all but one of the thirty-four correlations observed between the summary (i.e., not single-issue) indicators of party characteristics and the electoral system variables were positive, as expected, twenty-five of them significantly so. Many of the relationships were surprisingly strong, given the elusive nature of the concepts involved and the roughness of the measures available. Indeed, a majority of the thirty-four gammas (perhaps the more appropriate coefficient given marginal distributions that are constrained to be unequal) were greater than 0.50, indicating at least a three to one preponderance of nontied pairs of cases ordered in the expected, rather than in the unexpected, way.

The strength of these correlations is especially impressive in light of the obvious oversimplification implicit in the theory. There are at least three simplifications that, while perfectly consistent with the notion that politicians are rational actors and that party structures reflect that rationality, still would weaken the correlations observed here. First, it has been assumed that politicians are single-minded seekers of reelection. Yet, quite aside from acts of political heroism and self-sacrifice, most politicians have other goals that supplement, if not supplant, the desire to remain in office. Second, the electoral system has been oversimplified by treating each country as an undifferentiated whole, with each district implicitly assumed to have the characteristics of the "average" district. Yet, especially with regard to district magnitude, there can be substantial variation within a single nation.[23] Third, attention has been directed entirely at institutional variables in describing electoral systems, yet surely politicians might rationally respond to the predilections and desires of their electors, as well as to formal arrangements. What is impressive is that even after these simplifications have cut away the intricate complexity of real politics, and even with only forty-nine cases, significant statistical support regularly could be found for the hypotheses derived from the simple proposition that parliamentary deputies structure their parties so as to further their chances of reelection.

4

An Intensive Test: Electoral Experience

THE extensive test of the predictions based on electoral law revealed results that were clearly confirmatory. If some of the correlations observed were less than spectacular, many others were remarkably strong, especially in light of the simplicity of the theory and the quality of the data. In part, as illustrated by the problem of properly coding the intraparty preference vote in those systems in which it is available but not regularly important, the low correlations stem from the difficulties of operationalizing theoretical concepts consistently across widely varying systems without seriously distorting them in some systems. In part, as illustrated by the problem of PR with ordinal choice, the low correlations stem from the contradictory effects of two aspects of the same electoral law. In part, as illustrated by the inability to predict whether a party would be factionalized or fractionalized, they stem from the fact that electoral laws are only one part, albeit a major one, of the environment in which parties and candidates compete for office.

All of these problems are natural accompaniments of extensive tests of deductive theories. The solution, use of more sensitive analysis, requires the greater attention to detail characteristic of the intensive approach. In this chapter and the ones to follow, the theory developed in chapter 2, will be subjected to such a test, based on study of the Labour and Conservative parties in Britain, Fianna Fail and Fine Gael in Ireland, and the Democrazia Cristiana (DC) and Partito Socialista Italiano (PSI) in Italy.

Initial Predictions

This chapter is concerned with the actual operation of the electoral systems of the three countries, while the next focuses on campaign and nomination experience. In both, the analysis begun in chapter 2, will be extended and refined, and both the ultimate and the intermediate predictions will be subjected to test. Before beginning this intensive analysis, however, it will be useful to describe the electoral laws of the three countries to be considered, and to suggest the gross predictions that can be derived based on them alone.

British parliamentary elections are conducted under a system of single-member plurality voting. Each voter is given a ballot listing the names of a number of candidates; party is not mentioned on the ballot and indeed is unknown to British electoral law.[1] The only mark the voter may make without invalidating her ballot is a single cross next to the one candidate she wishes to support. At the end of the polling, the candidate from each constituency who has obtained the most votes is declared elected, regardless of how well other candidates in the district may have done.[2]

The British is thus a plurality system with categoric choice. Since each district returns only one member, the average magnitude of the districts in terms of voters per district and voters per deputy is the same, roughly 62,000 in 1970. Since each party nominates only one candidate in each district, and that candidate formally is selected by the party's members (actually in most cases by its local central committee), there is no intraparty choice by the average voter and candidates of the same party need not compete against each other for votes.[3]

Constituencies are large both in absolute size and in terms of voters per candidate; it therefore is to be expected that localism will be of little effect in campaigning.[4] Also because of the size of the constituencies, fairly extensive campaign organizations and reliance on mass media should be common. The single-member plurality system should lead to a contest focused almost exclusively between the top two candidates in each constituency, and the number of parties that are important in any way will be limited. Since these generally will not be the same parties in all constituencies, the campaign should take the form of a pragmatic appeal to the immediate policy concerns of the voters, rather than to complex or abstract ideologies. The number of issues of special relevance should be small, but because choice is categoric, issue positions should be articulated clearly. With no intraparty competition, there should be only one campaign organization for each party in every constituency and candidates should have no incentive to develop independent access to political resources. Alliances among parties are not to be expected, and should only take the form of the withdrawal of one challenger to the benefit of another. The expectation, therefore, is that British parties will tend to be issue oriented and cohesive, but not particularly ideological.

Elections in Eire are conducted under the single transferable ballot system. Again the voter is confronted with a list of the names of the candidates on her ballot, although here with the party affiliations of the candidates specified and with the likelihood that there will be more than one candidate from each party. Instead of indicating a single preference, the voter is asked to rank all, or as many as she wishes, of the candidates by writing the figure *1* next to her first choice, the figure *2* next to her second choice, and so on. (A cross next to a single name is also accepted as a valid *1* vote for that candidate if there are no other marks on the ballot, although then the vote would not be transferable.) After the voting, the valid votes are counted to determine the "total valid poll" for each constituency. If this is called N_i for the *i*th district, and that district is to return m_i deputies, the electoral (Droop) quota then is computed as the smallest integer greater than $N_i / (m_i + 1)$. This is the smallest number of votes that each of m_i candidates could receive while at the same time assuring that no other candidate could have as many. The ballots next are sorted according to the first preference votes marked on them and then are counted. Any candidate who has received at least as many first preference votes as the quota immediately is declared elected and his surplus is transferred to the remaining candidates in proportion to the distribution of second preferences expressed by the voters who gave him first preference votes.[5] If no candidate has more votes than the quota, the candidate with the fewest votes is eliminated and all of his votes are transferred to the remaining candidates according to the next available preference. If this gives some candidate more votes than required for election, he is declared elected and the resulting surplus is transferred from the last bundle of votes that he received. Otherwise, another candidate is eliminated. This process continues either until the required number of candidates have reached the quota or until there are only enough candidates remaining to fill the remaining vacancies, in which case they are declared "elected without having reached the quota."[6]

This system allows an ordinal choice by the voters; they may rank the candidates in whatever order they choose, either with or without regard to party. Party is, as under all plurality schemes, formally irrelevant, and in fact was not listed on the ballot until quite recently. In 1969 the average magnitude of the constituencies in terms of deputies per district was 3.5, with a range of from three to five deputies per district depending on population. The average number of voters per district was about 42,300; there were thus roughly 12,300 voters per deputy. Since the order in which candidates are declared elected is determined by the order in which they personally reach the quota, candidates of a single party are obliged to compete for votes against one another, as well as against candidates of other parties.

Given the small size of the Irish electoral districts and the generally rural character of the Republic, it is to be expected that localism will play a large role in campaigning and in voter decisions. When taken in conjunction with the ordinal choice offered the voters, this means that issues should play a relatively small role in campaigning. These characteristics, taken with the plurality electoral formula, should make ideology of little relevance to Irish politics. It is also to be expected that candidates will maintain independent campaign organizations and independent access to relevant resources, especially since a candidate's most direct electoral enemy may be another candidate of his own party. One therefore would expect that Irish parties will have relatively weak orientation toward issues, being instead concerned with questions of personality and especially with the provision of particularistic services to constituents. Whatever their ostensible level of cohesion with regard to matters of general policy, when concerned with the more important (to them) problems of patronage, the cohesion of Irish parties should be relatively low.

The Italian ballot is based on party lists rather than on individual candidates. The voter marks the single party that she most prefers. Within each district, the total number of valid votes and the total number of votes cast for each party are computed. The electoral, or *Imperiali* quota, then is determined by dividing the total number of valid votes by two more than the number of seats to be filled from that district. [N_i / (m_i + 2), to use the notation introduced for Ireland.] For each whole multiple of this quota contained in a party's vote, that party is awarded one seat. The remainders for any party that received at least one seat in any district are carried forward to the *Collegio Unico Nazionale* (CUN) along with any seats that have not been filled at the district level. In the CUN, the same process is repeated, although here the denominator in computing the quota is the number of seats to be filled from that district. [N_i / (m_i + 2), to use the tends to be much higher. The remaining seats are filled according to the largest remainder procedure. The particular individuals who are awarded their party's seats are determined by preference voting. After the voter chooses her party, she also is permitted to cite the names (or identifying numbers) of either three or four individual candidates from the party's list. Voters may not cast their *voti di preferenza* for any candidate of a party other than the one to which they have given their party votes, nor are they actually given the list of candidates in the polling booth; they must remember the names or numbers of the candidates for whom they intend to vote. Within each district, the party's candidates then are ordered according to the numbers of preference votes they receive (the ordering provided by the party has no effect except to break ties) and the seats awarded at the district level are assigned in this order. Seats awarded in the CUN are assigned to district party lists based on the size of the remainders transferred; such seats go to the next candidates on those lists.[7]

The Italian system is thus categoric with respect to parties; the voter may choose one and only one party. The magnitude of the districts is much greater than in either Britain or Eire, with an average of 19 deputies and 1,100,000 voters per district in 1972; in terms of voters per deputy, however, the average is about 60,000 voters, roughly equal to the ratio in Britain. The system is proportional among parties. The intraparty preference vote implies intraparty electoral competition.

The Italian electoral law leads to the expectation of ideological conflict among closely similar parties. It should not be surprising to find minor issues raised to a high ideological plane or to see a complex labyrinth of ideological positions emerge as a large number of parties try to maintain identities and compete for votes within a narrow ideological band. Without ordinal choice, and since the repeal of the *legge truffa* without bonuses for large votes, alliances among parties should be rare, short-lived, and perhaps even counterproductive. The size of the districts would tend to indicate a campaign conducted mainly through the media and through existing ancillary organizations, rather than by a small ad hoc campaign organization, although there may be a few candidates making localistic appeals in some areas. While candidates must attempt to have campaign organizations distinct from that of the party in order to compete for preference votes, the fact that each voter may cast more than one preference vote suggests that these organizations may exist to promote the candidacies of groups of candidates, rather than single individuals. Overall, then, Italian parties should be ideological in orientation, and either factionalized or fractionalized in operation.

Although electoral laws are extremely important, they do not describe a candidate's electoral circumstances completely. Indeed, even along those dimensions with which electoral laws are concerned, the laws themselves may not describe adequately the operation of any given system. For example, systems that are identical in legal terms may be more or less proportional in operation, depending on the way in which district boundaries are drawn and the way voters behave within them.[8] Deductions based on the propensity of plurality electoral laws to pit parties against different constellations of opponents in different districts are dependent on the degree to which this occurs. Whether it occurs is beyond the scope of formal law. Other dimensions of interest both to politicians and to political analysts lie even farther outside the legal realm.

Temporally the last, but logically the first, aspect of the electoral system requiring attention is the operation of the final, formal, electoral process. In considering the actual operation of elections in the three countries studied intensively, four facets of their performance will be considered in moving beyond the confines of formal electoral law:

1. the number of parties competing nationally and in each district, and the regularity with which the same parties compete against each other in different districts;
2. the patterns and relationships in turnovers of votes and seats among parties, in particular the proportionality of the electoral result;

3. the degree of nationalization of electoral change;

4. the use of the intraparty preference vote where one is allowed. Consideration of these variables will allow for more sensitive predictions concerning the structure and behavior of British, Irish, and Italian parties. The analysis also will allow the testing of many of the intermediate predictions suggested in chapter 2.

Before beginning this consideration, one preliminary comment is necessary. In specifying the relationships among various aspects of electoral law and candidate behavior, problems in assessing the direction of causation were minimal. In some cases electoral laws have been modified to reflect, or to be more appropriate to, established practice (for example the introduction of PR into countries that already have viable multiparty systems).[9] But from the point of view of the individual candidate at a particular point in time, electoral law may be seen as preexisting and essentially immutable. If there is any casual relationship between electoral law and candidate behavior, then the law clearly must be the cause and the behavior the effect. In the case of the variables introduced in this chapter, however, this is less clearly so. It will be argued, for example, that certain patterns of behavior are more appropriate to systems in which electoral change is highly nationalized than they are to systems with low levels of electoral nationalization. But, when such coincidence is observed, is it because the behavior of politicians produces the nationalization of electoral response, or because the politicians are responding to the predispositions of the voters? In all probability, if the lines of causation could be separated and measured, it would prove to be a bit of both. In any case, discussion in this chapter will tend to be in terms of coincidence rather than causation.

Number of Parties

At least on the surface, the most clear-cut of the variables to be considered here is the number of parties competing in elections; one should be able simply to count the number of party labels that appear on the ballots of the various constituencies. In fact, there are a number of questions that must be answered before a count may be made. In many polities, there are political parties that nominate candidates in only one or a few constituencies. Examples of this include the various parties that demand autonomy or union with a foreign state for particular regions as well as parties that make policy appeals that for cultural, economic, or demographic reasons are likely to be popular only in a few areas. Further, some candidates officially listed on the ballot as "independents" may be associated in some way with an existing party (for example the many "independents" in Japan who are in fact LDP members challenging incumbents and therefore denied their party's label),[10] or with a party that for some reason is unable to obtain official recognition.[11] Finally, the strength of a political party clearly determines its significance to a large extent. If access to the ballot is extremely easy, as it is in countries where a few signatures and a small monetary deposit are the only requirements for official nomination, the number of parties obtained by counting candidacies may vastly overstate the number of significant contenders. Put bluntly, where three parties competing in a single-member plurality election each have roughly one-third of the vote, there is three-party competition; when one party obtains 60 percent of the vote, a second 39 percent of the vote, and the third 1 percent of the vote, there is not.

These three problems all address the question, "When shall a party be considered a party—how widespread must its support be; how organized must it be; how strong must it be?" The answer to each aspect of this question is dependent on the level at which it is asked—national or local— and the use to which the answer will be put.[12] Since the concern here is with individual candidates, the questions will be asked at the level of single constituencies. A party will be counted in a constituency even if that is the only constituency in which it puts forward a candidate. This means that the number of parties competing may differ from constituency to constituency, or that even if the number of parties remains constant across geographic units, the actual parties making up that number may vary. It also means that the total number of parties competing within a nation may be greater than the greatest number competing in any particular constituency.

On the other hand, in the context of Western mass parties, an independent candidate is clearly different from the candidate of a party. This is because the party candidate, in accepting the party label, identifies himself with a political tradition and suggests that he will work cooperatively with others bearing the same label. Moreover, especially in parliamentary systems, he also accepts the proposition that the policy positions he takes, at least in deciding his legislative votes, in all but the most exceptional circumstances will be decided by some agency external to himself, whether that agency be the party leader, the parliamentary party caucus, or the party congress. Unless a candidate has some label that implies such commitments, he will not be considered a party candidate, although it will not be required that his party label be recognized officially. At the same time, it must be observed that in some cases independent candidacies may be both significant and successful.[13]

In deciding how strong a party must be to be considered significant, it is at a minimum clear that any party that elects one or more of its candidates must be considered among the parties competing in that constituency.[14] Further, any party that has a reasonable chance of electing a candidate must be included, or else every single-member district would have to be counted a single-party district. Even this, however, is inadequate. Suppose voters make their decisions strictly in accordance with a unidimensional, left-right, model of politics. Then suppose there are three parties, a leftist party with 42 percent of the vote, a center party with 40 percent of the vote, and a rightist party with 18 percent of the vote. Clearly, only the left and center parties have any significant chance of winning a single-member plurality election, yet to call this a two-party system fails to capture the tremendous significance of the rightist party. If it were to withdraw its candidate, the centrists would win every election easily. At least from the centrist point of view, there are three significant parties. Here, a party will be considered significant if it either elected a deputy or controlled at least as many votes as separated the weakest winner from the strongest loser. Thus, in a single-member district, a party was considered to be the only significant party if it won at least twice as many votes as its nearest competitor.

The number of parties competing in each district, and the number of different competitive constellations, or combinations of parties competing in different districts, are of interest because they figure in the derivation of predictions concerning the level of ideological concern parties are likely to display. To restate these arguments briefly, it was suggested that large districts (in terms of numbers of deputies per district) would encourage multiparty competition at the district level and that proportional representation would encourage both multiparty competition and the regular appearance of the same competitive constellation across districts. Multiparty competition and the appearance of few competitive constellations then were suggested to incline parties toward ideological behavior. These arguments are illustrated graphically in Figure 4.1.

From these arguments, two intermediate predictions regarding British, Irish, and Italian party systems may be derived and tested. First, there should be more significant parties in each constituency in Italy, with PR and very large districts, than in Ireland, with moderate size districts and plurality election, and more parties in Ireland than in Britain, with single-member plurality election. Table 4.1 reports the frequency distributions of numbers of significant parties for each of the three countries at each of the general elections held between the end of World War II and 1973, together with the mean number of parties per constituency for each election and the grand mean for each country. The grand mean for the British constituencies is just under two parties per constituency, that for the Irish constituencies is just under twice this at 3.77 parties per constituency, while the Italian grand mean (8.22) is more than twice that found for Ireland. Thus, the prediction is strongly confirmed.

Second, with its PR system, there should be fewer different competitive constellations found competing in Italy than in either Ireland or Britain. As Table 4.2 shows, this prediction also is confirmed overwhelmingly, especially if the obviously atypical Italian election of the *Costituente* in 1946 is ignored. The result is to reinforce the prediction that Italian parties

FIG. 4.1.
Graphic representation of relationship between electoral system
and ideological politics

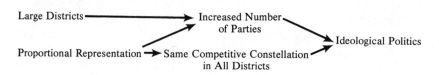

will behave ideologically, while those in Ireland and Britain will not, and particularly to increase confidence that if Italian parties are more ideological it is because of the influence of the electoral system.

Interparty Turnover and Proportionality

Any aspirant to, or incumbent of, parliamentary office must be concerned with patterns of vote distribution and turnover of seats both between and within parties, for these determine the candidate's initial electoral chances and the likelihood that he will retain his seat in successive elections. Implicit in the assumptions and analysis of chapter 2 was the notion that candidates of each party would tend to "rise or fall together." Where this is so, a high degree of "team" orientation on the part of a party's candidates is to be expected. For them to do otherwise would be to dissipate resources on nonproductive strategies. Different candidates may emphasize different aspects of their party's overall image; indeed it has been argued that this will tend to be the case under plurality electoral formulae, especially when there are single-member districts as well. Nonetheless, a good deal of campaign time may be devoted to associating the candidate with his party in the minds of the voters, attempting to improve the overall image of the party, and increasing the candidate's electoral chances *through* those of his party. On the other hand, when the individual fortunes of candidates tend to vary independently from those of the party overall, significantly less emphasis on party ties and party loyalty is to be expected.

In considering the degree to which a candidate's electoral chances are influenced by his party's aggregate electoral fortunes, the most obvious place to begin is with the proportionality of the electoral system. In this context, proportionality refers not to the electoral formula in the abstract, but rather to the degreee to which a party's percentage of the vote is equal to its share of the parliamentary seats, regardless of the formula by which this result is obtained.

At least to the extent that no democratic electoral system seeks to reward parties that receive grossly fewer votes with grossly more seats, [15] all

TABLE 4.1.
Frequency distributions of number of significant parties per constituency

nstituencies	Mean	1	2	3	4	5	6	7	8	9	10	11	12
						Number of parties							
at Britain													
1950	2.09	137	306	177	7								
1951	1.85	132	454	38									
1955	1.83	145	449	34	1								
1959	1.86	165	389	75	2								
1964	2.15	139	261	225	5								
1966	2.06	151	297	178	4								
1970	1.99	144	370	96	18	1							
Grand mean	1.97												
and													
1948	4.55		2	3	15	13	5	2					
1951	3.83		3	9	20	8							
1954	3.80		3	15	15	3	2	2					
1957	3.90		4	13	12	6	4	1					
1961	3.92		4	7	18	7	1	1					
1965	3.29		5	21	9	2	1						
1969	3.36		3	24	12	3							
1973	3.50		6	18	10	7	1						
Grand mean	3.77												
y													
1946	8.53					1	1	7	5	8	5	2	1
1948	7.67					1	1	12	12	2	1	1	
1953	8.27							1	20	9			
1958	9.35								1	19	10	1	
1963	8.03									30	1		
1968	8.19							2	24	5			
1972	7.52							15	16				
Grand mean	8.22												

electoral systems are proportional. Nonetheless, within this gross parameter, electoral systems may vary markedly in the degree to which they are proportional, both across time (from one election to another) and across space (from one country to another). Based on Rae's finding that the best predictor of proportionality is the number of deputies returned per district, it is no surprise to find, as demonstrated in Table 4.3, that the Italian electoral system is more proportional than the Irish, which, in turn, is more proportional than the British.[16]

In fact, however, the strength of the relationship between a deputy's chances of reelection and shifts in his party's electoral strength depends not so much on the overall proportionality of the electoral system as on the degree to which it treats marginal shifts proportionately. A system that rewards a party receiving roughly 60 percent of the vote with roughly 60 percent of the seats will appear proportional in aggregate terms, even if that party, in moving from 58 percent of the vote to 62 percent, loses seats. Yet to deputies seeking reelection, it is the latter notion of proportionality, by

TABLE 4.2.
Number of competitive constellations (N) by year

Great Britain		Ireland		Italy	
Year	N	Year	N	Year	N
1950	15	1948	12	1946	23
1951	9	1951	8	1948	5
1955	14	1954	12	1953	3
1959	16	1957	12	1958	5
1964	16	1961	11	1963	2
1966	16	1965	7	1968	5
1970	21	1969	3	1972	3
		1973	6		
Mean	15.3	Mean	8.9	Mean	6.6
				(1948–72)	3.8

which this system seems disproportional or even perverse, that is important. Here it is to be expected that the Italian system (with national pooling of remainders in the CUN) will remain proportional, but that incremental proportionality will be low in Eire (where patterns of transfers of votes may be as important as the initial distribution of first preferences) and in Britain. As the date in Table 4.4 show, this indeed has been the case.[17] Beyond the confirmation of this expectation, two additional observations may be made regarding these data. First, the British and Irish systems may be incrementally disproportional, and on occasion they are actually perverse. Between 1950 and 1951 the Labour party lost seats while gaining votes. The same fate befell Fianna Fail between 1969 and 1973, correcting in part their equally perverse gain in seats on a declining vote between 1965 and 1969.[18] Second, the gross change in the distributions of seats and votes in Italy has been very small in comparison to the other two countries.

Nationalization of
Electoral Change

Aggregate figures may mask some of the turnover actually occurring as a party's gains in one constituency are offset by its losses in another. If the party's vote rises and falls with relative uniformity throughout the country, this compensation is unlikely to occur. But, if voters respond to different issues in different areas, so that while the party is gaining votes in one set of constituencies it is losing votes in another, it is far more likely that the gross change will be greater than the net change observable in Table 4.4. As Table 4.5 shows, this in fact has been the case in all three countries.

Another way of looking at the same general problem is by measuring the degree of nationalization of electoral forces. In chapter 2 it was suggested that parties and their candidates operating in PR systems would tend to adopt the same ideological position in constituencies throughout the

TABLE 4.3.
Mean absolute deviation between parties' shares of seats and votes
(proportionality) by year

Great Britain		Ireland		Italy	
Year	Prop.	Year	Prop.	Year	Prop.
1950	3.9	1948	2.6	1946	0.3
1951	1.3	1951	1.5	1948	0.9
1955	2.4	1954	0.9	1953	1.0
1959	5.5	1957	1.8	1958	0.7
1964	5.3	1961	1.0	1963	0.8
1966	4.5	1965	0.9	1968	0.8
1970	2.2	1969	3.5	1972	0.6
		1972	1.6		
Mean	3.6	Mean	1.6	Mean	0.7

country, while under plurality systems candidates in different constituencies would adopt different, although not inconsistent, stands. If this is so, then one would predict that electoral change would be more highly nationalized in Italy than in either Britain or Ireland, and the test of this prediction becomes a partial test of the theory.

The average percentage of the variance in vote shares explained by national forces was computed for each of the six parties under study, at the level of constituencies for Great Britain and Ireland and at the provincial level for Italy.[19] Redistricting limited the Irish analysis to the four general elections held between 1948 and 1957,[20] and the British analysis to the five elections between 1955 and 1970. For both Italian parties the 1972 election had to be ignored since the provincial level data were not available, while for the PSI, the 1948 and 1968 elections had to be eliminated as well since the party was a partner in an alliance. For Britain, only those constituencies that were contested by both major parties at all five elections were considered. The results of this analysis are presented in Table 4.6 and clearly confirm this intermediate prediction.

Intraparty Turnover

Based solely on these results, one might be tempted to predict that party would be most important, and candidates most "team" oriented, in Italy. Such a prediction, however, would ignore the fact that there may be important turnover of personnel within parties even when no seats are gained or lost by them. These turnovers may occur for two reasons. In the first place, a sitting deputy may retire voluntarily, die, run for a different office, or be denied his party's nomination for a reelection bid. Although the literature on all three countries suggests that it is extremely rare for deputies wishing to be candidates for reelection to be forced out by their parties,[21] it is impossible to tell, especially after the passage of time, which retirements were voluntary and which were encouraged or even forced. This type of

TABLE 4.4.
Interelection changes (in percentages) in votes (dV) and seats (dS)

Great Britain			Ireland			Italy		
Elections	dV	dS	Elections	dV	dS	Elections	dV	dS
1950–51			1948–51			1946–48		
Conservative	4.5	3.6	Fianna Fail	4.4	7.1	DC	13.3	15.8
Labour	1.7	−3.3	Fine Gael	5.9	5.5	PSI	−8.7	−7.5
1951–55			1951–54			1948–53		
Conservative	1.7	3.3	Fianna Fail	−2.9	−6.1	DC	−8.4	−8.5
Labour	−2.4	−3.2	Fine Gael	6.3	5.5	PSI	6.8	8.2
1955–59			1954–57			1953–58		
Conservative	−0.3	3.3	Fianna Fail	4.9	10.7	DC	2.2	1.3
Labour	−0.6	−3.0	Fine Gael	−5.4	−6.2	PSI	1.5	1.4
1959–64			1957–61			1958–63		
Conservative	−6.0	−9.8	Fianna Fail	−4.5	−5.8	DC	0.8	0.8
Labour	0.3	9.4	Fine Gael	5.4	5.1	PSI	−0.4	−0.3
1964–66			1961–65			1963–68		
Conservative	−1.5	−8.0	Fianna Fail	4.0	0.0	DC	0.8	0.8
Labour	3.8	7.3	Fine Gael	0.2	−1.0	PSI	−5.4	−4.6
1966–70			1965–69			1968–72		
Conservative	4.5	12.3	Fianna Fail	−2.1	1.7	DC	−0.2	0.2
Labour	−4.9	−8.0	Fine Gael	0.2	1.9	PSI	0.2	−0.1
			1969–72					
			Fianna Fail	0.5	−3.8			
			Fine Gael	1.0	3.0			

turnover must, therefore, be ignored here. On the other hand, incumbents standing for reelection may be defeated, in which case it is clear from the official record and there can be little ambiguity as to what happened. In Britain, with single-member constituencies and one candidate per party, this can happen only if the incumbent's party loses the seat. In this sense, there is an absolute identity between the candidate's electoral chances and those of his party. In both Ireland and Italy, however, incumbents of parties that lose no seats, or even of those that gain seats, may themselves be defeated through the operation of the intraparty preference vote.

Table 4.7 reports the sources of turnover among incumbent deputies between pairs of elections in Ireland and Italy. Candidates were considered to have suffered "partisan" defeats if their losses could be attributed entirely to losses by their parties, that is, if no nonincumbents were elected; otherwise the loss was considered to be "intrapartisan."[22] In both cases, the intrapartisan losses are important. Indeed, for the Italian DC, only 2 of 140 defeats of incumbents were of the purely partisan type. For the PSI, even with far fewer seats per constituency and the consequently greater probability that the loss of a seat would force a partisan defeat, only about 26 percent of the defeats of incumbents were, in fact, partisan. For each party, intrapartisan defeats account for nearly half the total turnover among deputies. In the Irish case, intrapartisan defeats represent a bit under half (44 percent) of the defeats of incumbents, or 23 percent of the overall turnover of deputies.

TABLE 4.5.
Interelection gains and losses of seats

			Number of constituencies							
			Seats gained				Seats lost			
		Net change	4	3	2	1	1	2	3	4
Italy										
1953–58	DC	10		3	9	5		1		
	PSI	9		1	8	1				
1958–63	DC	−13				2	15			
	PSI	3			1	4	3			
1963–68	DC	5			2	5	1			
	PSI–PSDI	−29					1	16	5	1
1968–72	DC	1				6	5			
	PSI-PSDI	−1				4	5			
Great Britain										
1950–51	Conservative	23				24	1			
	Labour	−18				4	22			
1951–55	Conservative	23				29	6			
	Labour	−12				5	17			
1955–59	Conservative	26				30	4			
	Labour	−19				7	26			
1959–64	Conservative	−62				4	66			
	Labour	59				63	4			
1964–66	Conservative	−50					50			
	Labour	46				46				
1966–70	Conservative	77				79	2			
	Labour	−76				1	77			
Ireland										
1948–51	Fianna Fail	1				6	5			
	Fine Gael	9				10	1			
1951–54	Fianna Fail	−4				3	7			
	Fine Gael	10				12	2			
1954–57	Fianna Fail	13				16	3			
	Fine Gael	−10				1	11			
1961–65	Fianna Fail	2				5	3			
	Fine Gael	0				3	3			
1969–72	Fianna Fail	−6				3	9			
	Fine Gael	4				8	4			

Thus, despite the relatively high nationalization of electoral effects in Ireland, and especially in Italy, the electoral chances of Irish and Italian candidates, including incumbents, clearly appear differentiable from those of their parties. This leads to the prediction that candidates will be more "team" oriented with respect to their parties in Britain than in either of the other two countries. On the other hand, the prediction that team orientation will be greater in Ireland than in Italy must be avoided. While defeats of incumbents may be more common in Italy because of the nature of the electoral or party systems, the lower frequency of such defeats in Ireland may simply reflect greater conservatism on the part of Irish voters, or greater skill by Irish politicians in maintaining their positions. In any event, a fuller treatment of the preferential voting systems of Ireland and Italy is required before more detailed predictions may be made.

TABLE 4.6.
Percentage variance in vote shares explained by national factors

Great Britain		Ireland		Italy	
Conservative	56.6	Fianna Fail	58.3	DC	74.4
Labour	43.8	Fine Gael	60.3	PSI	67.6

Preferential Voting in Italy

Italian voters choose first their party, and only then may they select from its list either three or four of the candidates to whom they will give their *voti di preferenza.* The way in which this list is constructed will be discussed in chapter 5, but in considering the importance of the preference vote it is necessary to understand its basic morphology. In general, Italian party lists consist of three parts, any one or two of which may be missing from a given list. The first part consists of the one individual whose name appears first on the list, the *capolista.* After the *capolista,* there will appear on the typical party list a number of names ranked in the order of preference of the party's *direzione.* Taken with the *capolista,* this number generally sums to roughly the number of deputies the party expects to elect in that constituency. The final section consists of a number of names listed in alphabetical order. These names make the total length of the list roughly equal to the total number of deputies to be elected from the constituency. In other words, the list is much longer than the total number of deputies the party has any real hope of electing.[23]

The person selected as *capolista* is always a prominent party leader, either at the local or national level. It is the universal expectation that the *capolista* will lead the polling of preference votes within his party, and it may be reasonably interpreted as a great show of independence by the party electorate, or a serious misjudgment by the party leadership, if he does not do so. This is especially true because it is the expectation of party leaders that this interpretation will be made and they, therefore, devote a considerable effort to making sure that a person is not made *capolista* unless he will head his party's poll.[24]

The selection of the *capolista,* if it represents any communication at all, reflects the mass supporters of the party speaking to its leaders. The selection of the middle part of the list, however, reflects the party speaking to its followers. The party leaders are saying, in effect, "Here are the candidates we want elected, and here is the order in which we prefer them." If the preference votes cast leave this order unchanged, it does not necessarily mean that access to parliament is controlled entirely by the party leadership; it could be that the party leaders accurately anticipated the voters' preferences in constructing the list. However, if the voters fail to observe the list order either by changing the ranking of the candidates in the middle group or, more seriously, by electing candidates from the bottom

TABLE 4.7.
Interelection turnover of incumbents

| | | Defeated | | Not |
		Partisan	Intrapart.	candidate
Italy				
1953–58	DC	0	42	45
	PSI	0	12	17
1958–63	DC	2	35	36
	PSI	0	16	13
1963–68	DC	0	32	44
	PSI	3	12	36
1968–72	DC	0	29	41
	PSU as PSI	5	6	9
	PSU as PDSI	3	5	
Ireland				
1948–51	Fianna Fail	5	5	3
	Fine Gael	1	1	1
1951–54	Fianna Fail	5	4	12
	Fine Gael	2	5	12
1954–57	Fianna Fail	3	4	5
	Fine Gael	9	1	4
1957–61	Fianna Fail	8	1	11
	Fine Gael	1	2	11
1961–65	Fianna Fail	4	5	6
	Fine Gael	3	5	1
1965–69	Fianna Fail	1	1	12
	Fine Gael	3	3	7
1969–73	Fianna Fail	4	4	10
	Fine Gael	4	0	5

group while defeating candidates from the middle, this is evidence of autonomous decision.

If the party list order were the sole determining factor in the distribution of preference votes, and thus in establishing the order of election of candidates, the following hypotheses all could be confirmed:

1. When there is an individual who is *capolista,* he leads his party in polling preference votes.
2. Insofar as the number of deputies elected allows, no individual from the bottom category of the list is elected unless the *capolista* and all candidates in the middle part are elected.
3. There is a perfect correlation between the ranking on the party list of candidates in the middle part and their rank order in the polling of preference votes.

In fact, although list order clearly is related to the order of candidates' election, none of these hypotheses is verified by data for the DC and PSI taken from the 1972 general election.[25]

The data pertaining to the first two of these hypotheses are presented in Table 4.8, which reports for each party the numbers of individuals from each of the three sections of their party's list (1) who headed the polling of

TABLE 4.8.
Italian electoral result by list position, 1972

	DC electoral result			PSI electoral result		
List position	Headed poll	Elected	Defeated	Headed poll	Elected	Defeated
	Number elected greater than number ranked					
Capolista	12	0	0	9	1	0
Middle	0	61	15	0	4	1
Bottom	0	48	135	0	20	309
	Number elected equal to number ranked					
Capolista	8	3	0	8	2	0
Middle	3	69	9	1	6	3
Bottom	0	9	115	0	3	184
	Number elected less than number ranked					
Capolista	4	1	0	3	0	1
Middle	1	42	20	1	0	3
Bottom	0	4	49	0	0	41

their party for preference votes, (2) who did not head the poll but were elected, or (3) who were not elected in constituencies in which the number of candidates ranked by the party (*capolista* plus middle section) exceeded, equalled, or was less than the number of deputies actually elected. Since any deviation from a perfect correlation is statistically significant, no significance test was performed on these data. It may be seen, however, that in four of twenty-eight cases for the DC (14.3 percent) and in four of twenty-four cases for the PSI (16.7 percent) the *capolista* did not, in fact, head his party's poll, and indeed in one case for the PSI, the *capolista* actually was defeated while another PSI candidate was elected. Likewise, even when the number of ranked candidates was smaller than the number actually elected, in each party roughly 20 percent of the middle category candidates were defeated. Further, when the number of ranked candidates exactly equalled the number of deputies elected, 11 percent of the middle category DC candidates and 30 percent of the middle category PSI candidates were replaced among the elected by individuals from the bottom category of the list. Even in the third case, when more candidates than could be elected were ranked, and in some sense therefore endorsed by the party, four bottom-category DC candidates managed to secure election.

The final hypothesis could be tested only for the DC because the length of the ranked portions of the PSI lists, reflecting the number of deputies the party might hope to elect, was too short for meaningful rank order correlations to be computed. Inspection of Table 4.8 suggests, however, that there is no reason to suspect that the result would differ significantly. Table 4.9 reports the frequency distribution of Kendall's tau, computed at the constituency level, between the ranks of candidates as expressed on the party list and their actual order as determined by the preference voting.[26]

Although the results are due in part to the shortness of the lists, it is interesting to note that sixteen of the twenty-seven correlations are *not significantly different from 0 at the level of p < 0.05,* notwithstanding a prediction of perfect correlation.

Because the length of the list would seriously affect the weight given to each constituency in computing an overall statistic, constituencies were divided into two categories, those with from five to nine individuals, and those with from ten to fifteen individuals, on the middle parts of their DC lists. Within each category a Spearman's r was computed for the entire category. For the long lists, this was found to be 0.43, while for the shorter lists it was 0.51. Since confidence intervals may be computed for this statistic, it may be asserted with 95 percent confidence that, for the long lists between 6 percent and 33 percent of the variance in the final rankings by preference voting may be explained by party list order and for the shorter lists between 11 percent and 42 percent of the variance may be explained in this way. More importantly, it is clear that over one-half, and probably closer to three-fourths of the variance in the order of election is determined by factors other than party list order.

Having said this, it still must be asked how Italian voters in fact do decide upon the candidates for whom they will cast their preference votes. The first thing that must be said in response is that to a great extent they do not decide; that is, they simply do not cast their preference votes at all. As Table 4.10 shows, the result found by D'Amato for earlier Italian elections still obtains:[27] well under half the possible preference votes are in fact cast, and while there is important regional variation, in no constituency are more than about 65 percent of the possible preference votes cast.[28] This means that relatively few preference votes are actually necessary for election. In the DC, candidates require the preference votes of only about 10 percent of their party's voters to be elected (on average about 31,000 votes). Candidates of the PSI have tended to require a somewhat larger share of their party's electorate, about 18 percent, but this translates into fewer actual supporters (on average about 18,000). Moreover, the margin between the last elected and the first defeated candidates often is no larger

TABLE 4.9.
Frequency distribution of Kendall's tau between list order and electoral order for middle section of DC lists, 1972

	Number of correlations
Tau < 0	3
0 < Tau < 0.2	5
0.2 < Tau < 0.4	8
0.4 < Tau < 0.6	3
0.6 < Tau < 1.0	8
Total	27

than a few hundred votes. Again, there is a good deal of regional variation, with more preference votes (representing a larger percentage of the party electorate) needed for election in the South, but the overall pattern of few preference votes being required for election persists in all sections of Italy. To the extent that endorsements of local organizations and local leaders can influence votes, such endorsements should be particularly valuable. First, the absolute size of the consistuencies makes it impossible for a candidate personally to influence enough voters to secure election. Second, the proportion of the party electorate required is small enough for a single endorsement to be significant. This, in turn, suggests that there are a small number, but a number greater than one, of *independent* resource bases adequate for election to the Chamber of Deputies.

To what extent are endorsements significant in influencing preference votes, or more generally, how do Italians who cast preference votes choose the candidates they support? Two bodies of data may be brought to bear on this question. First, D'Amato not only tabulated the frequency with which the preference vote is cast by party and by region, but also reported on a survey of Italian voters that asked those who claimed to have cast preference votes in the 1958 election the criteria they used in deciding for whom to vote. The results for the PSI and DC are reproduced in Table 4.11. The minimal importance of party is reflected in the fact that fewer than 18 percent reported having followed their party's advice. Much more important were those who reported either knowing the candidate (more likely knowing of him) or having heard of him informally. This is in keeping with the two-stage flow of information that has been found in other contexts,[29] but it does little to explain why the good things that these voters heard pertained to one candidate rather than to another. Unfortunately, D'Amato did not ask about the influence of group affiliations, which in fact are extremely important (see below, especially chapter 5).

Elite perceptions of the facts are as important to the arguments made here as the facts themselves. Further, given the two-stage flow of information, these perceptions may be a more accurate source of system-level information than survey responses. Therefore, Italian respondents to the questionnaire used in this study were asked to estimate the importance of each of

TABLE 4.10.
Preference votes cast in Italy as a percentage of total possible, 1968

Region	DC	PSI
Northeast	27.6	14.7
Northwest	26.9	19.0
Center	28.6	17.4
South	56.7	48.8
Islands	56.4	46.7
Nationwide	39.5	28.5

TABLE 4.11.
Reasons for candidate choice given by Italians casting preferences votes in 1958 (by percentage)

	DC	PSI
I follow the advice of my party	15.1	17.7
I follow the advice of my *corrente*	8.2	6.2
I know the candidate	24.9	27.3
I heard the candidate well spoken of	23.7	13.9
I read in the newspapers that they were the best	5.4	7.7
I heard one of their speeches	2.5	5.7
I saw them on TV	1.3	2.9
I prefer to vote for someone who I believe represents my party *corrente*	6.1	7.7
I give my preference vote to someone who has been or will be helpful to me	11.2	8.4
Other	1.2	1.9
No response	0.4	0.9

Source: Luigi D'Amato, *Il voto di preferenza in Italia* (Milan: Giuffre, 1964), table 56.

seven factors in determining the particular candidates voters support with preference votes. (For information regarding sampling and the question-naire used in this study, see Appendix A and Appendix B.) These factors are listed in Table 4.12, together with the percentages ranking each factor as either "Very Important" or "Important" on the one hand as opposed to "Not Very Important" or "Irrelevant" on the other. As might be expected of individuals operating in very ambiguous circumstances, there appears to be great reluctance to assign a low level of importance to any factor. Nonetheless, important differences emerge. Consistent with D'Amato's result, the degree to which candidates are known and the candidates' previous political experience (which is basically another way of saying the degree to which they are known) rank highly along with their personal political views. Also consistent with D'Amato, endorsement of national party leaders and *corrente* rank at the lower end of the order, with residence ranking last. In light of what has been said concerning the impact of the low level of preference voting, it is extremely significant that the most important factor (and indeed the only factor that was not ranked as "Irrelevant" by even one respondent) is the endorsement of local party leaders.

Preference Voting in Ireland

The only way in which an Irish party institutionally could endorse some of its candidates in a way analogous to the list order in Italy would be to nominate only as many candidates as it could elect in each constituency. If parties could, would, and did do this, they clearly would control access to parliament. As Table 4.13 shows for the 1973 general election, however, this is rarely the case. In fewer than 17 percent of the constituencies for Fianna Fail, and in fewer than 5 percent of the constituencies for Fine Gael, did the Irish parties present exactly the "right" number of candidates; in all other cases they presented at least one, and in one case as many as three,

TABLE 4.12.
Reasons for candidate choice given by candidates and party officials in Italy (by percentage)

	Very Important or Important	Not Very Important or Irrelevant
Tha candidates' policy views	71	29
The candidates' residence	37	63
The candidates' political experience	71	29
The endorsements of national leaders	54	46
The endorsements of local leaders	87	13
Difference in the degree to which candidates are known	71	29
The candidates' *corrente*	50	50

more candidates than they elected. Thus, the significance of the preference vote is clear. It remains to be seen how regularly Irish voters make use of this facility and the criteria upon which they decide the order in which they will rank candidates.

The degree to which Irish voters make use of the intraparty choice allowed them may be assessed in either of two ways, both of which show that they do, in fact, use this facility overwhelmingly often. Chubb computes the percentage of the total vote that eventually becomes nontransferable.[30] For the 1969 general election this figure was 5.8 percent. This may make too generous an estimate, however, since many votes are never scrutinized for transferability. Looking only at those votes that are considered, however, the result stands. Of those votes scrutinized after the first count fewer than 10 percent are in fact nontransferable.[31]

The Irish preference vote need not be used only within a single party. It is therefore important to ask whether the preference vote is used primarily as an intraparty preference or as an interparty mechanism for ranking candidates. If it is used predominantly as a mechanism for expressing a

TABLE 4.13.
Frequency distribution of number of candidates and elected deputies per constituency, Ireland, 1973

	Number elected		
Number of candidates	1	2	3
1 Fianna Fail			
Fine Gael			
2 Fianna Fail	3	7	
Fine Gael	16	2	
3 Fianna Fail	12	18	
Fine Gael	15	7	
4 Fianna Fail		1	
Fine Gael		1	
5 Fianna Fail		1	
Fine Gael			1

TABLE 4.14.
Transfers of votes, Ireland, 1969 and 1973 (by percentage)

		Party transferred to				
		Fianna Fail	Fine Gael	Labour	Other	Non-trans.
Party transferred from		(with candidates of same party remaining)				
Fianna Fail	1969	79.9	6.5	5.2	1.3	7.1
	1973	87.8	1.1	2.9	1.7	7.1
Fine Gael	1969	7.6	77.9	6.6	1.4	6.6
	1973	3.3	75.1	10.0	0.8	10.9
Labour	1969	9.5	11.7	70.0	2.3	6.6
	1973	4.7	16.4	72.3	2.1	4.4
		(with no candidates of same party remaining)				
Fianna Fail	1969		21.8	11.7	12.3	54.2
	1973		27.2	20.1	1.8	50.9
Fine Gael	1969	17.7		28.5	1.6	52.3
	1973	28.1		28.1	.4	43.5
Labour	1969	13.7	32.1		5.9	48.4
	1973	7.8	71.1		5.9	15.2

choice within party, then the great preponderance of votes should transfer from one candidate to another of the same party, provided a candidate of that party remains. Table 4.14 reports these figures for the three major Irish parties from the 1969 and 1973 elections. In both cases, over three-fourths of the votes do transfer within party when possible, and of those that do not, many become nontransferable. When it is not possible to transfer votes within party, however, Irish voters do use the preference vote to express a preference among the alternative parties (confirming that choice is, in fact as well as in form, ordinal). As the table shows, while over 50 percent of the Fianna Fail votes become nontransferable once there is no Fianna Fail candidate remaining, roughly half of the Fianna Fail and Fine Gael votes, and over half of the Labour votes, do go to other parties when they cannot remain with their own.

Table 4.14 is also significant in illustrating the point made in chapter 2 regarding ordinal choice and electoral alliances. In 1969, Labour and Fine Gael were not allied; in 1973 they were allied, and were victorious even though they polled relatively fewer first preference votes than they had in 1969. Very little change took place in the distribution of transfer votes while there was still a candidate of the same party left. Once there was no party candidate, however, the Labour party delivered 71 percent of its transfer votes to Fine Gael candidates in 1973 as opposed to 32 percent in 1969, while giving Fianna Fail only 8 percent instead of 14 percent. In other words, with no loss at all to themselves, the Labour party was instrumental in electing additional Fine Gael deputies to the detriment of Fianna Fail.[32]

How then do Irish voters choose among candidates of their party in order to rank them? Paul Sacks has provided the answer for at least one Dail

TABLE 4.15.
Reasons for candidate choice given by candidates and party officials in Ireland (by percentage)

	Very Important or Important	Not Very Important or Irrelevant
The candidates' policy views	61	39
The candidates' residence	79	21
The candidates' political experience	89	11
The endorsements of national leaders	57	43
The endorsements of local leaders	46	54
Differences in the degree to which candidates are known	82	18

constituency—by locality. Although Irish election results are reported formally only by constituency, they are tallied informally by party poll watchers to establish the distribution of first preference votes by polling booth. Sacks analyzed these informal records for the 1969 election in Donegal North-East, and found that the best predictor of vote was the distance from the polling booth to the candidate's home. In fact, for the two Fianna Fail candidates, it was possible to draw a short straight line through the constituency such that one candidate had over 50 percent of the party vote in every polling booth on one side of the line, while the same was true for the other candidate on the other side of the line. While the relationship was not quite so strong for the Fine Gael candidates (a situation partially explained by the fact that one was a Protestant and the other a Catholic in this border constituency), the relationship was, by social science standards, overwhelming.[33]

These data come from only one constituency, but the trend is accepted generally by Irish politicians as being true throughout the country, with the exception of the borough constituencies of Dublin and Cork. One interview respondent, for example, reported that he owed his election to the fact that, "I was the first candidate of either party ever nominated from the——— peninsula."

Table 4.15 reports the responses of the Irish respondents to the question "Could you rate the importance of each of the following in determining the order in which voters support the candidates of a single party in your constituency?" As was true with the Italian respondents to the questionnaire, the findings are consistent with previous research. The most important factor appears to be the candidate's political experience, which, as Sacks reports, can significantly increase the size of his bailiwick.[34] The second most important factor is related to the first and is the degree to which the candidates are know. Again consistent with Sacks, the third most important factor is the candidate's place of residence. This factor was the least important in Italy, but is most important of all in Ireland if the Dublin respondents are eliminated. The policy views of the candidates, the endorsements of national leaders, and particularly the endorsements of local leaders (the most important factor in Italy) are less important in Ireland.

The overall result of this analysis is to reinforce the predictions suggested at the beginning of the chapter. In particular, it is to be expected that campaigns will be more nationally oriented in Italy than in either Britain or Ireland, but that the "team" orientation of candidates, and by extension of deputies, will be greatest in Britain. The prediction that Irish and Italian candidates will maintain separate campaign organizations has been reinforced, but it can be made more specific. In detail, Irish candidates are expected to emphasize locality and personal independence in campaigning, while Italians are expected to appeal for local group and personal endorsements, and to emphasize their attachments to such groups or individuals.

5

An Intensive Test: Campaign and Nomination

PRECEDING the balloting stage of an election, but primarily conditioned by expectations of voter behavior and the effects of the application of electoral laws, are the nomination and campaign stages of the electoral process. In considering campaigns and nominations, this chapter has two objectives. First, by bringing under consideration additional aspects of the environment in which candidates seek office, the argument from electoral system to parliamentary party structure will be advanced and sharpened; new predictions will be made, and general predictions made in previous chapters will be made more specific. Second, the strength of the arguments made to this point will be increased by the partial verification of several of the intermediate predictions relating to campaign behavior deduced from them.

In keeping with the practice of working backwards, the requirements and techniques of campaigning will be considered first. This section will begin by considering the predictions concerning the nature of campaign appeals made in chapters 2 and 4, showing that reported practice conforms to the predictions. Based partially on this analysis, the techniques of campaigning and then more importantly the resources required for the effective employment of these techniques will be discussed. Finally, from the conclusions of this part and consideration of the distribution and availability of electorally relevant resources, predictions will be made concerning the behavior of deputies.

The same basic strategy also will be followed in discussing nominations. Three questions will be addressed: first, what is relevant to the selection of candidates; second, how can candidates influence the selection process; third, what implications does this selection process have for candidates' behavior once they are in office?

Campaigning

Journalistic accounts of politics and formal (particularly spatial) models of politics both attribute great importance to the role of issues in political campaigns. They suggest that the policy proposals of parties that gain votes over previous elections and especially the policy proposals of parties that win a majority of the votes have been endorsed by the public, while those of parties that lose votes have been rejected. As has been suggested, this is a dangerous assumption for a number of reasons, two of which may be singled out as being of particular relevance in this context.[1] In the first place, while all parties make policy appeals to voters, these appeals are not the only factors that influence the electorate. Even leaving aside the independent impact of party identification in determining a large proportion of the vote in some countries, and considering only fluctuations in voting strength, it is clear that the personalities and other characteristics of both national and local party leaders and candidates may have an impact independent of, and perhaps greater than, that of the policy differences between the parties. In the second place, even when policy appeals are important in influencing voters, it is far from self-evident that the same issues will be important in different areas. Yet, unless this is true, it is difficult indeed to interpret electoral results as referenda on any particular issues.[2]

What, then, can be said of the impact of issues in campaigns in Italy, Ireland, and Great Britain? How important are issues? What types of issues, and what specific issues, are stressed by parliamentary candidates? Do different candidates stress the same or different issues? Answers to these questions have been predicted in the preceding chapters, based first on deductive analysis of the electoral laws of the countries involved, and second on a combination of deduction and induction from an analysis of the electoral experiences of the three countries since World War II. The task now is to confront these predictions with data in order to see whether the line of reasoning that produced them can be confirmed.

Based in part on considerations of district magnitude and in part on the nature of choice allowed voters, it has been suggested that issue appeals will be of greater importance in Italy and Britain than in Ireland. Respondents to the questionnaire (Appendix B) were asked to rate the importance of national and local issues and national and local leaders in determining the result of the immediately preceding general election in their constituencies. While these data must be interpreted with some caution because it became clear that there was no way to force the Irish and Italian respondents to distinguish between the result with respect to parties and the result with respect to individuals, it is still possible to assess the relative importance of issues in the three countries. Table 5.1 reports the percentages of the respondents from each country reporting the opinion that national and local issues and leaders were "Very Important" in determining their constituencies' outcomes. Comparisons regarding the importance of "national issues" test the hypothesis most directly and are in the expected directions. British and Italian respondents rated these issues as considerably more important than

TABLE 5.1.
Importance of national and local issues and leaders in determining
constituency electoral results

	Percentage reporting factor "Very Important"		
	Great Britain	Ireland	Italy
National issues	77	36	66
National leaders	27	50	21
Local leaders	12	18	25
Local leaders	9	32	21

did the Irish. At the same time, the difference between Italian and British respondents is large as well.[3] Also within the category of national factors, the issue orientation hypothesis is confirmed by the ratio of the percentage attributing importance to "national issues" to the percentage attributing importance to "national leaders." This ratio is between 2.8 and 3.2 for the British and Italian respondents, but less than 0.8 for the Irish. While the intercountry differences for "local issues" are too small to be of importance, the "local issues" to "local leaders" ratios are as expected, again indicating greater issues orientation in Britain and Italy than in Ireland.

The difference between the British and Italian respondents appears to be the result of two factors. First, the Italians appear to be confusing the partisan result with the personal one; this should increase the importance attributed to local leaders. Second, given the great stability of partisan voting in Italy,[4] it may be that each factor has less impact in Italy than in Britain or Ireland.

It also was predicted that candidates of a single party would tend to stress the same national issues to a greater extent in Italy than in either Britain or Ireland. This prediction was partially confirmed when it was found that electoral change was most highly nationalized in Italy. This finding might lead to the expectation that national issues would be most important in Italy and of lesser importance in Britain and Ireland, but Table 5.1 shows that this is not the case. The finding also gives rise more directly to the expectation than Italian candidates will be more likely than British or Irish candidates to stress national issues in their campaigns, a prediction that is concerned with candidates' choices rather than with their environments. The candidates sampled (both elected and defeated) were asked whether they had stressed national or local issues in their campaigns. The responses to this question are reported in Table 5.2. The direction of the differences confirms the hypothesis that national issues will be stressed more heavily in Italy (100 percent). Unexpectedly, however, the British candidates overwhelmingly report having stressed national issues in their campaigns as well (88.7 percent).

Further reflection allows this to be explained partially. Low electoral nationalization, and nonideological politics, can be brought about in either

TABLE 5.2.
Candidates stressing national or local issues in campaigning (by percentage)

	Great Britain	Ireland	Italy
National issues	89	39	100
Local issues	11	61	0

of two ways. On the one hand, candidates and voters may pay particular attention to local issues and personalities. This appears to be the case in Ireland. On the other hand, they may pay particular attention to national concerns and still bring about a low level of electoral nationalization if different candidates and their respective electorates pay attention to *different* national issues. Apparently, this is the case in Britain. Responding candidates were asked to cite the one or two particular issues to which they had devoted the greatest attention. Those issues cited by significant numbers of candidates are listed in Table 5.3. While the issues stressed naturally differ from country to country, the significant difference is in the shapes of the distributions. No more than 28 percent of the British respondents mentioned any single issue, but nearly 93 percent of the Italians mentioned specifically having stressed "my party's program." While this is a fairly vague response, it does suggest first that there was important similarity within party in what Italian candidates were saying, and second that, as predicted on the basis of electoral formula, what they were saying was complex and multidimensional. In particular, it reflects that fact that, unlike their British counterparts, Italian candidates, while attempting to tailor their campaigns to specific audiences, find it virtually impossible to focus only on one issue to the exclusion of others. This tendency also is reflected in the fact that, rather then mentioning education or social services separately, the Italians lumped these together under the general category of "social reform." (Another interesting aspect of these data is that while large numbers of both British and Irish candidates reported stressing "social services," the British regarded this as a national issue while most of the Irish respondents considered it to be local.)

Politicians' opinions concerning the ways in which voters may be influenced are important for a number of reasons. Such opinions are of interest here primarily because they determine the resources that candidates will perceive themselves to require. When taken with the distribution of these resources in the political system, candidates' perceptions of their needs influence the types of accommodations and connections they are likely to form in order to gain access to resources. As a result, these opinions also affect candidates' behavioral styles not only in the narrowly defined area of campaigning, but also in the wider parliamentary arena.

All respondents to the questionnaire were asked to rate the importance of a number of campaign techniques in influencing voters in their constituencies.

TABLE 5.3.
Candidates stressing various issues in their campaigns (by percentage)

Issue	Great Britain	Ireland	Italy
Law and order	14	0	0
Education	8	0	0
Economic position of country	22	18	7
Social services	28	41	0
Honesty to pledges	6	0	0
Industrial relations	8	0	7
Taxation	6	12	7
Social reform	12	0	21
Defense and foreign affairs	6	0	0
Inflation	18	0	0
Employment	10	24	14
Regional policies	8	0	0
Stability of government	0	24	0
"My party program"	0	0	93

These techniques are listed in Table 5.4 together with the percentages in each country who rated them "Very Important" or "Important." (The Italian respondents were not asked to rate personal canvassing.)

Based on the relative district magnitudes, it was predicted that media-oriented campaigns would be more important in Britain and Italy than in Ireland, an expectation that is confirmed by the relative ratings for television and radio, although this is regarded as an important campaign technique in all three countries. In all three, television and radio campaigning is the province of the national party, since national leaders are far more likely than backbenchers or simple candidates to be considered newsworthy in the general run of events. Moreover, the time allotted specifically to campaigning on the state-owned and controlled broadcast media is given to the parties and not to individual candidates.[5] Therefore, the use of the radio and television campaigning ought to have a nationalizing influence in all three countries, and may account in part for the high level of electoral nationalization in these countries when compared to the United States.[6] To the extent that broadcast campaigning is relevant to individual candidates, it should tend to reinforce the existing pattern of power within the national party, since it is a campaign resource to which access is controlled by the national party leadership. Access to television and radio probably will be divided in whatever way the party's leaders tend to divide other things of value—cabinet posts, nominations, etc.

Speeches by national leaders also were considered important in all three countries and again are controlled by the national leadership. In part, these speeches are influential because they are carried over the airwaves and reported in the national press; to this extent, the leader finds it hard to distinguish among candidates and, other than having some nationalizing impact, these speeches should have little effect on candidate behavior. Beyond this, however, the speeches of national leaders can offer benefits to

TABLE 5.4.
Campaign techniques rated "Important" or "Very Important" by respondents
(by percentage)

Technique	Great Britain	Ireland	Italy
Television and radio	86	68	79
National newspaper endorsements	44	57	50
National newspaper advertising	24	46	37
Local newspaper endorsements	44	57	71
Local newspaper advertising	24	57	29
Speeches by national leaders	83	89	67
Speeches by local leaders	49	68	67
Personal canvassing	78	100	—

particular candidates. By appearing in a constituency, a party leader gives special support to the candidates of his party in that area. Even more, by appearing on the same platform with a particular candidate the leader lends him special support. In the absence of other evidence, it must be presumed that the support of national leaders is one resource in which candidates will be interested.

It was predicted that personal factors would be especially important in Ireland because of its small constituencies and ordinal choice. This expectation is confirmed by the fact that over 95 percent of the Irish respondents rated personal canvassing as a "Very Important" campaign technique, as compared to 52 percent in Britain. This difference between Ireland and Britian also may be explained by the fact that canvassing is one of the few acceptable ways in which Irish candidates may appeal directly for votes for themselves as well as for their parties—a problem that British candidates do not face. In the organization of canvassing, the pattern of bailiwicks that Sacks found in analyzing the vote is reproduced to an even greater extent.[7] When two counties are included in the same constituency, each party is likely to maintain two completely separate campaign organizations.[8] Further, within rural constituencies, each candidate has his own area within which he is expected to concentrate his campaign. For example, in an often cited report, the *Dundalk Democrat* quoted one candidate complaining that a fellow candidate "was putting canvassers into the Carrickmacross area to help . . . have him defeated. . . . 'It speaks badly for a candidate who is forced to leave his area where the people know him.'"[9] More generally, over two-thirds of the non-Dublin respondents mentioned "areas near [their] residence" when asked to describe the areas in which they had concentrated their campaigns. The exceptions were typified by the respondent who reported that he had made an arrangement to divide his constituency in his first campaign only to be defeated by a few hundred votes after another candidate invaded his territory a few days before the polling. For Irish candidates, this reinforces the pattern of independent bases of electoral support commented upon earlier. For both Irish and

British candidates, the importance of canvassing means that volunteer workers should be an important campaign resource.

Respondents in Ireland and Italy rated speeches by local leaders as important. For the Irish, this is of little interest since the local leaders in question are almost always the candidates themselves. In the Italian case, however, there are both candidates who are not important local leaders and important local party leaders who are not candidates. Here, the support of local elites must be regarded as an important resource, although in both the Irish and Italian cases, respondents may have been referring more to intraparty than interparty choice when they rated this factor so highly. Likewise, the support of local, regional, and organizational newspapers is a valuable resource in Italy, but not in Ireland or Britain (where the local press is much weaker and less likely to make endorsements). The importance of these two resources emphasizes the observation that there are a small but significant number of independent bases of support in Italian constituencies.

In all countries, money is clearly important to the mounting of an effective campaign. The amount necessary varies from one country to another, however. In Ireland, the importance of money in campaigning is limited by the small size of the constituencies. Because so much of the campaign is personal, because radio and television time is either free or unavailable, and because local newspapers that sell advertising space are both inexpensive and published infrequently, an Irish party or candidate has very little on which to spend money. As a result, every Irish respondent estimated the total cost of his party's campaign, including the individual expenses of all candidates, to have been under $12,500, even in the five-seat constituencies and even in Dublin. Extrapolating from the distribution of responses, and making the most generous estimates possible, the cost per candidate of the major parties is computed at less than $1,800.[10] The importance of money in Britain is limited by legislation. Until 1974, when the limit was raised, no candidate could spend more than £ 450 plus 1 1/2 d. per voter in the borough constituencies or 2 d. per voter in the county constituencies, plus £ 100 for personal expenses. As a result, the average cost per candidate for the major parties is well under $5,000.[11] In Italy, on the other hand, campaigns are far more expensive. It has been estimated that the cost per candidate in the 1972 general election was over $16,000,[12] and since this figure includes both candidates of minor parties with little financial support and candidates from the bottom of party lists with no real chance of election, the average cost per serious candidate of a major party must be at least five times this amount.

The figures for Ireland and Italy include the cost of the party campaign and the cost of each candidate's individual campaign. As has been seen, however, these are clearly separable given the importance of the intraparty choice. For this reason, candidates in Ireland and Italy were asked to estimate the cost of their own, personal, campaigns. As the results, tabulated in Table 5.5, clearly show, money is a far more important resource for Italian candidates than it is for the Irish.

In terms of campaigning, then, the important resources for British candidates are the support of national party leaders and the services of large numbers of volunteer workers. In Ireland, the same resources are necessary, although the smaller district sizes may reduce the actual number of volunteers required. In addition, candidates in rural constituencies require a territorial base of support. For the Italians, volunteers are far less important but money, local press endorsements, and the support of local and national leaders are potentially important. The degree to which these actually should affect candidate behavior and the particular consequences brought on by the need for these resources depends on the degree to which they are mobilizable and the ways in which they are distributed within the system.

The endorsement and support of national party leaders is a potentially significant resource in all three countries. In examining the way in which this resource operates in the three countries, however, three distinct patterns emerge. British candidates are not in competition with their copartisans for the support of the national leadership. In the first place, the direct aid of these leaders is becoming difficult to mobilize. With the rapid expansion of television campaigning, front bench politicians, and particularly the prime minister and leader of the Opposition, are increasingly concentrating their campaigns in television studios and making fewer forays into the con-stituencies.[13] As a result, it is only the less influential leaders who are available at all for local campaigning. Further, when these leaders do campaign in the constituencies, they tend to choose the places to which they will go on the basis of the electoral advantage of the party as a whole rather than to aid particular individuals. This means that they tend to concentrate on a few marginal constituencies spread widely across the country. When they speak, they address national problems and speak for the national party, only incidentally supporting the local candidate. This trend has only been strengthened by the concentration of media and public attention on the potential prime ministers.

In contrast, Irish and Italian candidates might be in competition with each other for the support of national leaders since they are in competition with each other for votes. In Ireland, however, this is ruled out by the party leaders themselves. While the Taoiseach (prime minister) and opposition leader campaign extensively, they tend to cover all constituencies rather than selecting a few as in Britain. When they speak in the constituencies, they are extremely careful not to show any favoritism toward one candidate, and indeed all candidates of the party will appear on the platform with their leaders. The personal campaigns of Italian party leaders are also extensive.

TABLE 5.5.
Candidates' personal campaign costs (by percentage)

Personal campaign costs	Ireland	Italy
$0 to $1,250	78	11
$1,250 to $6,250	22	11
$6,250 or more	0	78

Here, however, they are far less even-handed, and do in fact support individual candidates.

These differences are reflected in the questionnaire data. Table 5.6 gives the percentages by country reporting that one or more national party leaders had campaigned in their constituencies at the time of the preceding general election. Under one-third of the British respondents reported such campaigning, while roughly one-half the Italians and three-fourths of the Irish reported having a national party leader campaign in their constituencies. The degree to which the campaign in Britain is concentrated in a few constituencies is illustrated by the fact that of those Britains reporting a national leader having campaigned in their constituencies, roughly one-half reported that at least one other national leader had done so as well, while the corresponding figures for the Irish and Italians were one-third and one-fifth, respectively.

The difference between the styles of the Irish and Italian leaders is shown by the way Irish and Italian respondents describe the object of their leaders' local campaigns. Every Irish respondent described the campaign appearances of national leaders as being for the benefit of all candidates of the party. In contrast, nearly one-half of the Italians (46 percent) reported that the campaign appearances of their national leaders were for the benefit of some particular candidate. Overall, then, the support of individual national party leaders is a resource for which Italian candidates must compete while this is not the case for either the British or the Irish.

In recruiting campaign workers, British candidates need not adopt a competitive stance vis à vis other candidates of their own party. The campaign is organized at the constituency level, but there is only one candidate per party in each constituency. The local party's professional agent administers and plans the campaign, while the local party organization provides the funds (and more importantly the volunteers) required for effective campaigning. Indeed, both major parties limit even the amount of personal money that a candidate may spend. The degree to which recruitment of workers can be left to the constituency party is illustrated by the response of one MP to the question, "About how many people were actively involved working in your campaign in the last general election?" He replied, simply, "I don't know. That is my agent's responsibility and I leave that entirely to him." Roughly 20 percent of the British respondents gave similar answers to this and another question about campaign costs, as

TABLE 5.6.
Respondents reporting at least one and two or more national leaders campaigning in their constituencies (by percentage)

Number of national leaders appearing	Great Britain	Ireland	Italy
At least one	32	75	46
Two or more	15	21	8

compared to no Irish "Don't Knows."[14] The pattern of autonomous local resource bases for Irish candidates is reflected in the fact that over half the Irish respondents mentioned "my area of the constituency" when asked from where their campaign workers had been recruited (compared to 96 percent of the British respondents citing their constituency parties).

Three resources have been suggested as potentially important to Italian candidates—funds, the support of local newspapers, and the endorsements of local and national elites. In fact, the way in which these resources are organized tends to bring the last to particular prominence and to suggest that the most important resource for an Italian candidate is the support, whether direct or through the mediation of another individual, of one of the major national interest groups that contribute to his party's coalition.

Some Italian newspapers such as *Avanti!* and *Unita* are controlled by political parties, which means in fact that they are controlled by a subgroup of party leaders. Other leaders will control other periodicals or press agencies, such as *Politico, Forze Libere,* or *RADAR* in the DC. Interest groups or business combines may operate daily newspapers as well, as illustrated by the National Hydrocarbon Trust's (ENI) *Il Giorno* in Milan or the Vatican's *Osservatore Romano.* In other words, access to and support by the press is controlled by a limited number of leaders with direct partisan interests.

Likewise, a small number of leaders control the support of volunteer workers and the contribution of funds. The overwhelmingly important source of these resources for British candidates is the constituency party. For the Irish, it is local party cells within the constituency. But for the Italians, organizations such as Catholic Action, the Italian Association of Christian Workers (ACLI), trade unions, and Confindustria are likely to channel significant resources to a limited number of candidates who have been particularly favorable to their interests.[15] (While such national interest groups as the Confederation of British Industry, the Trades Union Congress, and the National Farmers' Union all make political contributions in Britain, these go almost exclusively to the national parties for national campaign expenses and so are of little direct relevance to individual candidates. A partial exception is the sponsorship of candidates in the Labour party.)

Taking this discussion together with the hypotheses tested in this chapter, it is possible to make some more specific predictions about the parties under study. Since British candidates do not have to compete against one another either for votes or for resources (which are in fact provided by the local party) and since the orientation of local party activists (at least during the period under study here) is know to be strongly toward loyalty to the national party leadership,[16] it is to be expected that British parties will conform well to the norms of cohesion and issue orientation, but will not adopt an ideological style. Given the tendency of campaigns to focus on a few, different, issues in different constituencies, there may be significant disagreements within British parties on some issues. What is particularly important, however, is that the party, in dealing with other parties, will do so as a cohesive entity.

In Ireland, the predominating influence is territoriality. Each candidate has his own personal base of votes and resources; issues are of far less importance. Hence, it is to be expected that the principal orientation of Irish politicians will be toward cultivating and maintaining their local support and, while Irish parties will be cohesive with respect to policy, they will not be clearly divided with respect to policy differences. Instead, each deputy will operate primarily as an independent entrepreneur in the procurement of particular benefits for his constituents.

Finally, in Italy the overwhelmingly important resource is the support of one of a limited number of national interest groups and their leaders. As a result, it should be expected that Italian parties will be composed of ideologically or policy oriented factions based on the support of and access to special interest groups, mediated by factional leaders.

Nominations

Before the interparty electoral campaign can begin, each party must select the particular individuals who will represent it. In most cases, and in the case of each of the six parties studied here, this is strictly an intraparty decision, in which neither government nor nonparty groups may participate. Many objectives are pursued in the nomination decision, for example, rewarding loyal party work or financial support, but clearly the aim that predominates in the overall process is the desire to win elections. Thus it is to be expected that the patterns observed here will reflect and reinforce those based on electoral law and its operation and on the requirements of campaigning.

In each of the countries studied, the nomination procedures used are basically the same for all parties. In Britain, the selection of candidates is the jealously guarded prerogative of the constituency party organizations, although in all cases the national party exercises a formal veto, either before or after local selections. When a constituency party wishes to choose a new candidate, an announcement is made and a list of possible candidates is drawn up. In the Conservative party, individuals may apply directly. Labour party candidates must be nominated by some affiliated organization, but since it would be the rare candidate who could not secure the endorsement of some trade union branch or ward party this is not a significant difference. This list then is narrowed to a short list by a committee of local party leaders and from the short list a final selection is made. In the case of the Conservative party the name is submitted to the association membership for final ratification.[17]

Irish party nominations are made by constituency conventions to which each local branch is entitled to send delegates. After the number of candidates to be selected is decided, nominations are accepted from the floor and the actual selection is made by election, using the single transferable ballot method. Before nominations are made official, they must be approved by the national party, which provides the chairman of the constituency convention and unlike British parties makes regular use of its power to veto individual candidates and to impose additional nominees on the constituency party.[18]

The Italian nominating process is composed of four basic phases. First, names of prospective candidates are proposed by local and provincial party organizations. Next, the number of names is pared down by a constituency level party committee. Third, the tentative list is ordered. Finally, the list is sent to national party headquarters where the ordering of the list is made final. At this stage, names also may be added or deleted from the list. In all parties, the central *direzione* makes relatively frequent use of its power to alter the list order and, in particular, to impose a *capolista*.[19]

While each of these nominating procedures leaves open considerable choice of the criteria by which candidates are selected, in fact the fit between the requirements and practices of campaigning and the choice of candidates is quite close. This may be demonstrated through the testing of three hypotheses.

   1. British candidates will be chosen as effective spokesman for their national parties. Local considerations will be of little importance as will be individual support of party leaders from outside the constituency.

This is not to minimize the fact that nominations are controlled locally and that the prejudices of local elites are therefore overwhelmingly important. It suggests, however, that these generally will not be prejudices for candidates with local connections.

   2. The predominant requirements for nomination of candidates in Ireland will be local connections.

Reflecting the need for a local power base, Irish candidates may frequently hold local office within their constituencies simultaneously with standing for or serving in the Dail.

3. The selection of Italian candidates, and their favorable placement on their parties' lists, will be influenced most strongly by their support by national or local leaders of groups within or associated with their parties.

The lack of localism in British nominations may be seen most simply by looking at the residences of candidates. Responding candidates were asked whether they lived in the constituencies for which they stood, and if so, for how long they had lived there. These data, reported in Table 5.7, show that while roughly 90 percent of the Italian and Irish candidates had lived in their constituencies for over ten years (in fact, almost all had lived there all their lives), over 70 percent of the British candidates had never lived in their constituencies and several who did report living in their constituencies said that they had moved there only after being selected as candidates. The lack of importance placed on local ties also is reflected in the fact that the typical MP will have stood unsuccessfully in one or more different constituencies before finally being elected.[20] This process of "shopping around" for a constituency is particularly important because it minimizes the impact of the only area in which serious intraparty conflict might arise and might lead to disunity. Unlike the United States, for example, where residence within the constituency virtually is required for nomination, in Britain the unsuccessful candidates for nomination in one constituency may be adopted in another. Thus, there need be no unequivocal defeats and hence no fierce and disruptive competition. For example, two of the British respondents to the survey reported here, who are now good friends, originally both sought nomination from the same constituency. When one was selected, the other simply applied to a nearby constituency and was adopted there.

All respondents were asked to rank the importance of a number of factors in the selection process. The percentages ranking each factor as most important are shown in Table 5.8. This table reinforces the point just made regarding the lack of importance placed on local contacts by British candidates; fewer than one-sixth of the British respondents ranked local contacts as most important as opposed to 32 percent of the Irish and 38 percent of the Italians. (Only 34 percent ranked local contacts among the top three factors as compared to 70 percent for Ireland and 61 percent for Italy.) Instead, the most important factors were previous political experience and personality; indeed, over two-thirds of the British respondents listed *both* of these factors among the top three. The third factor that appears important is the political views of the prospective candidate, ranked first by 16 percent and among the top three factors by 67 percent of the British respondents. On further probing, this was shown to refer primarily to views consistent with party policy and not to differences among individuals within the party. Endorsements by both individuals and groups are unimportant, except that 24 percent of the Labour party respondents (as opposed to no

TABLE 5.7.
Residence of candidates (by percentage)

	Great Britain	Ireland	Italy
Does not live in constituency	72	11	14
Has lived in constituency less than ten years	9	0	0
Has lived in constituency more than ten years	19	89	86

Conservative respondents) ranked group backing among the top three factors. This is the one significant difference between the two parties of the same country found in this study. Even here, however, British respondents ranked other considerations more highly, reflecting the fact that there is competition among sponsored candidates. In general, it may be concluded that British parties are looking for attractive candidates only. Individual views, attachments, and support are of minimal importance.[21]

For Irish candidates, the same complex of variables that dominates the distribution of preference votes is crucial to the determination of nominees. The data in Table 5.7 suggest most powerfully the impact of localism; the only candidates who did not report living all their lives in their constituencies lived and stood for election in Dublin, but in different constituencies. When asked to rank the factors important to nomination, only three factors were given any considerable support—constituency contacts, experience, and the endorsement of local leaders. All three of these point directly to the importance of a local power base. Indeed, when taken with the lack of support for other factors, these data illustrate clearly that the *only* way to secure nomination is to have an individual local base of support. Further probing reveals that the party leaders referred to are the secretaries of local branches in the prospective candidate's area of the constituency. Experience means service on local government councils, which every candidate had, and which two-thirds of the deputies continued after election. Previous research has shown clearly that this service is valued primarily because it allows the candidate to build a personal following based on the dispensing of patronage.[22]

The greatest difference between Italian respondents and those from Britain and Ireland is the importance accorded to group support. Again, personal views are of little importance, although significantly respondents here seem to be referring to shades of opinion within the party and not simply to support of the party line. The most important factor, constituency contacts, seems to refer particularly to connections within ancillary organizations and interest groups associated with the party. In other words, where British parties try to select the best spokesman for their positions, in a process rather like actors' auditions, and Irish parties seek to achieve geographic balance between individually powerful local leaders, Italian party nominations reflect the relative power of organized groups. Thus all three hypotheses are confirmed by these data.

TABLE 5.8.
Factors ranked as most important in selection of candidates (by percentage)

	Great Britain	Ireland	Italy
Constituency contacts	16	32	38
Previous political experience	23	36	17
Trade union or other group backing	5	0	21
Personality	22	0	4
Candidate's political views	16	4	-8
Support of party leaders	8	25	8

In terms of candidate strategies, the first significant conclusion to be drawn is that there is nothing the prospective British candidate can do beyond building a record of party loyalty and service over a period of time. Being sponsored, as opposed to not sponsored, may help a Labour candidate in some constituencies, but with a few exceptions, mostly in mining areas, the identity of the sponsoring body tends to be irrelevant. The Monday Club's attempt to influence nominations in the Conservative party was an almost complete failure.[23] Responding party officials were asked whether any of the candidates for nomination had done anything to influence the selection process and if so what effect that action had had. Very few prospective candidates attempted to influence the process and most significantly, those who did were hurt by their actions and very infrequently selected. Several responding officials also volunteered that they had warned prospective candidates against canvassing the nominating committees and that if they had done so it would have hurt them. In sum, then, the British nominating procedure both reflects and supports the already existing tendency to party unity.

For Irish and Italian candidates, the situation is different. This is illustrated partially by the fact that while two-thirds of the British candidates reported themselves to have been "self-starters," two-thirds of both the Irish and Italian candidates said that their candidacies had been initiated by party leaders or groups. The Irish candidate is part of a local organization. Frequently, he will "inherit" candidacy from a retiring local politician. Canvassing local leaders before the nominating convention is a common practice; over 57 percent of the Irish respondents reported canvassing or being canvassed as compared to 17 percent in Britain. Since the maintenance of an organization based primarily on patronage is essential to nomination, it is to be expected that once elected deputies will be strongly motivated in this direction. While canvassing is not important for Italian candidates (only 12 percent reported canvassing or being canvassed), this is because the actual decisions are made by committees on which the groups supporting the prospective candidates already are represented. The crucial job facing would-be Italian candidates is to maintain their support. Since these groups are largely local branches of hierarchically controlled national organizations (which in turn are represented on the national committees that finally approve and order the constituency lists), this provides a firm basis for factionalism, again reinforcing the tendency already predicted on the basis of more immediate electoral considerations.

6

An Intensive Test: Verification

IN the preceding chapters, the electoral systems of Great Britain, Ireland, and Italy have been examined in the light of a theory of candidate rationality to the point at which specific predictions have been made regarding the nature of parliamentary parties in these countries. This chapter concludes the intensive test by doing two things. First, the process by which these predictions were reached will be reviewed briefly for each country. Second, the actual nature of the six parliamentary parties studied will be described so that it may be seen that the predictions made are, in fact, accurate. In doing this, only those aspects of the parliamentary parties that are relevant to the predictions will be considered. Since these predictions have dealt with broad characteristics, these discussions will not require the wealth of detail expected in single-party or single-nation studies and may, therefore, initially appear somewhat superficial. The differences among the parliamentary parties of the three countries studied are so large, however, as to make relatively gross comparisons adequate for the purpose of showing that the equally gross differences predicted by the theory presented here obtain in the real world.

Britain

A British parliamentary candidate is selected primarily as a spokesman for his national party. So long as he is prepared to defend his party and its platform before the electorate and to support the party's leaders on divisions in the House of Commons, the candidate personally may oppose them on some issues. The candidate's personal strength within the party, or the support of prominent party leaders or interest groups are of little effect in securing nomination, and indeed even a former cabinet minister sometimes has trouble finding a constituency. At the same time, the intensity of his conflict with other would-be candidates is moderated by the fact that those not selected in one constituency may be adopted in another.

Once adopted, the candidate campaigns in an environment that is again oriented toward party. British voters make their decisions in terms of party; although the ballot lists only candidates, and not parties,[1] and although the personalities of the national leaders may have a significant impact on voter choice, it is universally conceded that the local parliamentary candidates influence at most several hundred votes. The resources the candidate needs are procured for him by the constituency party, which in most cases will organize his campaign as well. The orientation of the electorate toward party, together with the size of the constituencies, leads to concentration on issues, and these tend to be national. Because of the effects of the single-member plurality electoral law, this leads to the prediction that British parties will conform well to the norms of cohesion and issue orientation, but will not be ideological.

The Conservative party readily can trace its history back to the Tories of the eighteenth century and continuously has been identified with the traditional forces in British society, the aristocracies first of birth and then of wealth, the established church, and the empire. The Labour party arose from the movement of the late nineteenth and early twentieth centuries to secure direct representation in Parliament of working people by working people, and rose rapidly to replace the Liberals as the country's second party, providing the classic example of the "squeezing" of a center party in a single-member plurality system.[2]

In terms of the social bases of their support, the two major British parties are different, but not overwhelmingly so. The Labour party is a working class party; 75 percent of its voters are self-described members of the working class. On the other hand, while the Conservative party is the strong choice of the upper and middle classes, because of the relatively smaller numbers in these classes, over half of its supporters are working class as well.[3] Thus, the class orientation of the parties is tempered by the fact that each party must have significant support from more than one class if it is to be victorious. The class basis of the party system does not, therefore, as it might under an electoral system more favorable to such competition, lead to ideological conflict between a Marxist party and a capitalist one, notwithstanding the fact that the Labour party is nominally socialist and many of its members are themselves Marxists. At the parliamentary level, the class differences between the parties have become progressively smaller as more Labour MPs, and especially more Labour cabinet ministers, come from university backgrounds while fewer Conservatives come from the leading public schools.

Rather, if there is an underlying philosophical difference between the British parties it is probably that the Conservatives favor a meritocratic society (perhaps with the implicit assumption that merit is hereditary) while Labour stresses the need for equality, especially of opportunity, even if this involves substantial leveling downward. In neither case are these more than vague orientations, and in neither case do they lead to an ideological political style.[4] In neither case is any substantial ideology offered to support either general value preferences or particular policy stands; in neither case is there complete internal agreement on policy, strategy, or values within party or disagreement between them; in neither case are policy stands immutable over time.

Neither party presents its policy proposals as the logical consequence of a general theory of society. Indeed, the Conservatives do not even have an official statement of goals in their constitution, and while the Labour party does, it is at such a level of abstraction as to be of little practical use.[5] Rather, ideology serves a symbolic function without playing any important role in practical politics.[6]

On most issues, a majority of the electoral supporters of one party agree with a majority of the supporters of the other; this is true in most countries. What is significant, and indicative of the nonideological nature of British political competition, is that even on the question of nationalization, the only issue that has divided the parties continuously since the war,[7] and one of the issues that most sharply divides them today, the parties are far from unanimous.[8] While the differences among MPs are larger, there is still significant overlap between the parties and disagreement within them.[9]

That the choice of issue positions by British parties is not governed by ideological considerations is illustrated in two ways. First, rather than supporting their own parties' proposals, the leaders of British parties tend instead to attack their opponents. Thus, in 1970, 75 percent of Harold Wilson's major speeches were devoted to attacking the Conservative opposition, while Edward Heath devoted 70 percent of his time to attacks on the Labour government.[10] In general, the concern is tactical, rather than ideological. Illustrating this even better is the frequency with which some of the major policy positions of British parties change. Writing in 1974, Richard Rose observed that since the Conservatives returned to office in 1970,

A majority of Labour MPs have voted against entry to the Common Market, against a Conservative prices-and-incomes policy, and against an Industrial Relations Act, even though they had supported such policies while their party was in office. Similarly, the Heath government abandoned opposition to a prices-and-incomes policy, accepted the withdrawal of British troops from East of Suez, and refused a compromise Rhodesian settlement, going against views previously held by a majority of Conservative MPs.[11]

Similarly, when Harold Wilson was prodded in a parliamentary question in December 1965 to explain why the Labour government was not making greater progress toward British entry into the E.E.C., he silenced Conservative opposition by saying,

Entry into the E.E.C. is not open to us in existing circumstances and no question of fresh negotiations can arise at present. We shall work with our E.F.T.A. partners through the Council of Europe, and through W.E.U., for the closest possible relations with the Six consistent with our Commonwealth ties.

He was quoting, but not citing, the 1964 Conservative election manifesto.[12]

If the policies of the major parties are chosen for tactical reasons and if they are altered frequently, the resulting differences are nonetheless real at any given time. A comparison of the positions taken by the two major parties in their 1970 election manifestos shows disagreement on seventeen of eighteen issues examined.[13] While these positions may change between the election and the meeting of Parliament, the parties remain divided; on over 95 percent of the divisions in the House of Commons, nine-tenths or more of one party oppose nine-tenths or more of the other.[14] Indeed, the norm of united party facing united party is so strong that a single defection on a division may have serious consequences for an MP, while the defections of as many as twenty or thirty MPs may, under some circumstances, cause the fall of the party leader.

Within each party, there are a number of subgroups based either on shared interest in, but not necessarily agreement on, particular policy areas—committees on defense, Commonwealth affairs, nationalized industries—or on a generally shared view with regard to party policy.[15] The former type are of interest because they illustrate the importance of policy to British MPs; in Ireland, it would be difficult to find enough deputies with sufficient interest in policy to staff even a skeletal version of the British committee system. The latter type, notably the Friends of Tribune in the Labour party and the Bow Group, PEST, and the Monday Club in the Conservative party, are of interest, and conform to the predictions, because they have not developed into the kinds of intraparty factions that characterize Italian parties. This is illustrated by the fact that most British MPs answered "no" to the question, "Are there any groups within your party that tend to stick together behind a particular leader?" while every Italian deputy responded "yes." While some leaders are more prominent in these groups than others, the crucial point is that they are unable to enforce discipline, as is demonstrated by the failure of the Monday Club to expel Geoffry Rippon even though as a member of the government he has been responsible for policies opposed by the Monday Club, and unable to speak for the entire membership in any authoritative way. Most importantly, it would be unthinkable for leaders of these groups to negotiate across party lines to undermine a government. In each case, the aim of the groups has been to influence party policy by stirring up discussion and convincing the leadership rather than by attempting to replace the leaders of the party.[16] Much of the activity of both types of groups is informal and private, aimed at promoting consensus, rather than being openly conflictual. This is particularly true with regard to the doctrine of collective responsibility as applied to the government (which includes up to one-third of the ruling party and precludes any open disagreement with its program). Again, this contrasts strongly with Italy.

There are also a number of select committees of the House of Commons as a whole, the most notable being the Select Committee on Science and Technology. This committee has had considerable success in investigating and reporting on a number of topics, especially nuclear reactor policy, with members showing considerable nonpartisan independence, and developing substantial expertise. The success of committees of this sort again reflects the policy interest of members of Parliament. At the same time, the norms of party unity have been preserved by the rigid exclusion of such committees from any field that could threaten the government of the day. This is well illustrated by the decision to disband the Select Committee on Agriculture, even though it had not been particularly critical of government policy, when it insisted on investigating an area that the government considered to be sensitive.[17] All this suggests strongly that British parliamentary parties are policy oriented, although not ideologically so, and cohesive, as has been predicted.

Of course, British parties are not perfectly cohesive, as the continuance of such groups as the Monday Club and Friends of Tribune shows. Embarrassing parliamentary questions frequently are asked by members of the minister's own party. An analysis of Early Day Motions has shown that a number of groups with diverse views exist in both parties.[18] Members of select committees, of both parties, have been on occasion critical of government policy. Nonetheless, it is crucial to understanding the nature of British parliamentary parties to note that these forms of expressing dissent almost always are used to persuade during the early stages of policy formation. Once party policy has been set, virtual unanimity in support of it may be expected, particularly at the stage of divisions, whether required by party rules (as in the case of the Labour party) or not.[19]

The character of representation by British MPs is suggested by their responses to two further questions asked in connection with this study. First, each was asked to specify his area of particular expertise, if he felt that he had one. In each country, roughly 20 percent of the respondents replied that they had no special area of knowledge. The British respondents, reminiscent of the diversity of issues raised in their campaigns (see Table 5.3), were distinguished, however, by the breadth and variety of the responses made. Fewer than 20 percent mentioned any particular area, and the remaining responses were spread over the entire range of government policy, including defense, shipping, mining, and policy toward developing countries, as well as the more common social services, education, and labor relations. MPs also were asked to identify what they considered the single most important aspect of their jobs. As is shown in Table 6.1, these responses split roughly evenly between the provision of service to and representation of the grievances of local constituents on the one hand, and the formulation of public policy on the other. This duality of focus also is documented by MPs' use of parliamentary questions, which divide between attempts to redress individual or local grievances and attempts to criticize or illuminate general public policy, with significant numbers of questions in each category.[20]

Ireland

The overwhelmingly important criterion in the selection of Irish candidates is the support of the party branches in their local areas of their constituencies. Unlike the British case, a candidate who fails to secure adoption in one constituency has virtually no chance in another, in which he would have no local connections. Would-be candidates are thus immediately in competition with one another for the scarce resource of local support.

Once candidates are selected, the same situation obtains. While funds are not terribly important, they are supplied primarily by local party branches; the same is true of campaign workers. Candidates of the same party must compete against each other for the first preferences of party supporters, and again this competition is organized locally, with each candidate concentrating his efforts in the area of the constituency in which he lives and from which the bulk of his support at the nomination stage is drawn as well. Thus it was predicted that, while Irish parties might be cohesive with respect to policy, they would not be divided clearly by policy differences. Instead, each deputy will operate primarily as a free agent in the procurement of particular benefits for his constituents.

The division between Fine Gael and Fianna Fail dates clearly from the split in the Sinn Fein party over acceptance of the 1922 treaty with Great Britain establishing the Irish Free State within the British Commonwealth. Those who accepted the treaty formed the Cumann na nGaedheal party under the leadership of W. T. Cosgrave; the antitreaty forces organized a third Sinn Fein party, and then in 1926 formed the Fianna Fail party under the leadership of Eamon de Valera. Until 1927, when faced with a law requiring all candidates to pledge to take their seats if elected, the antitreaty deputies abstained from the Dail, allowing Cosgrave, with fewer than 50 percent of the Dail seats, to form three successive governments and remain in power until 1932. In 1933, the Fine Gael party was formed in a merger of Cumann na nGaedheal, the Center party, and the proto-fascist Blueshirts, with General O'Duffy as leader. By 1935, Cosgrave had returned to the leadership, and the party could be seen quite clearly as the lineal successor of Cumann na nGaedheal.[21]

Since the founding of the Irish Free State, this cleavage has been reinforced by periodic repression, or perceived repression, of one party by the other, and transmitted by heredity. The sons of four of the ten ministers in Cosgrave's first government were ministers in the Fine Gael-Labour coalition government formed in 1973, including Cosgrave's own son as Taoiseach; also in 1973, the sons of Fianna Fail's first two Taoiseachs, de Valera and LeMass, were Fianna Fail deputies. Over one-fourth of the deputies elected in 1965 had family connections with former or sitting deputies.[22] Sons frequently "inherit" their fathers' seats in the Dail.[23] Particularly in the case of Fianna Fail, the continuing crisis in Northern Ireland has provided vivid illustrations of the persistence of this cleavage, with four ministers resigning or being sacked for complicity in an arms running scheme,[24] while a Protestant Fine Gael deputy lost his seat in 1973 as a result of a mildly pro-IRA remark.

More significantly, no new issue has arisen to distinguish the parties, to the extent that it long seemed likely that both parties would ally themselves with the same group in the European Parliament.

The main parties have usually issued party programs, sometimes in very general terms. When social and economic matters loomed large in the 1965 election, all the parties produced programs and plans, but since to most people they must have looked very much alike, it is doubtful whether they swung many votes or made much impact. . . . The only persistent theme of recent years has been an institutional one, the desirability of one-party government as against coalitions.[25]

Indeed, in the last several general elections, Fianna Fail's principal issue was that it was the only party capable of forming a government; its loudest boast is that it draws its support equally from all segments of society. While Fine Gael is more clearly the party of the middle class and large farmer, it is by no means exclusively so, and its alliance with the more heavily working class Labour party further negates any sociological distinction between the parties. Differences between the parties on policy questions have been exclusively matters of minor detail;[26] on all recent important issues—public security and the suppression of the IRA, entry into the Common Market and policy within it, amendment of the constitution to further reconciliation with the North, easing the ban on contraceptives—the parties have either been in agreement or else taken no clear position.

Notwithstanding the almost complete lack of policy distinction between the parties, they behave with extreme cohesion in the Dail on matters of policy. Decisions taken by the party caucus are binding and deviations from the party position not infrequently result in expulsion from the party.[27] This has been particularly true in Fianna Fail as the governing party and as the party with a more deeply ingrained tradition of revolutionary loyalty. At a deeper level, however, this unity is somewhat illusory, for it is the unity neither of people in agreement nor of people willing to accept defeat on important issues by partisan colleagues. Rather, it is a unity born jointly of disinterest in policy and the recognition of the patronage benefits resulting from party control of the government. Decisions are taken by very few party members, or simply by the leader, not because of their great power, but because nobody else either cares strongly or feels qualified to question their decisions. As Basil Chubb has noted, "In general . . . the position of governments does not rely to any extent upon sanctions. Rather, it rests upon strong feelings of loyalty and a considerable willingness on the part of the ordinary TD to let his party leaders get on with what he regards as *their* business of government and opposition, assured of his support, while he attends to *his* business, notably constituents."[28]

At the same time, deputies, particularly of the ruling party, recognize that party unity is to their private advantage. The problem facing the Taoiseach, and especially the leader of the opposition, is not how to handle competition for office or front bench positions, but how to find enough members with even minimal qualifications who are willing to serve.[29] One-fifth of the Irish deputies (TDs) responding to the questionnaire reported that they had either held and resigned or else refused junior ministerial or front bench opposition posts. The parties appear united because in a parliamentary system that is how they may compete most effectively for power. They desire power, however, not because it would enable them to alter policies but because it gives them greater access to patronage.

The indifference of Irish TDs to policy may be illustrated by their responses to the question, "What is the single most important part of a TD's job?" Only 7 percent responded that developing policy or legislation was most important. (See Table 6.1.) If policy is not important to TDs what then is? Again looking at Table 6.1, the answer is clear; over 85 percent responded that the single most important part of their jobs was the promotion of particular constituency interests or the provision of services to their constituents. This emphasis on local service also is demonstrated by the fact that Irish deputies use their parliamentary questions almost exclusively to press for local interests or personal benefits for constituents, and even more frequently simply to demonstrate for home consumption their interest in local problems even when parliamentary intervention is entirely unnecessary.[30]

On the subject of providing local services, Irish parties are not cohesive at all; rather, they are made up of independent entrepreneurs, each out to do as much as he can for as many individual constituents as possible, and to take credit in as large an area of his constituency as possible for things that often would have happened anyway.[31] This emphasis on localism also is underscored by the fact that fully 50 percent of the responding Irish deputies

TABLE 6.1.
Deputies' responses to the question, "What is the single most important part of a deputy's job?" (by percentage)

	Great Britain	Ireland	Italy
Constituency service	32	86	0
Developing policy	39	7	82
Overseeing government	7	0	0
Knowing his constituency	7	0	0
Other	16	7	18

cited "local government" as their principal area of expertise and is reflected in the fact that a majority serve simultaneously as county councillors. Moreover, a larger proportion of Irish than of either British or Italian respondents (28.6 percent as opposed to 16.1 percent and 18.2 percent, respectively) felt there was no area of policy in which they were expert. Further, even those deputies who do take an interest in policy areas other than "local government," are far different from their British counterparts, who typically specialize in one area of policy in which they develop expertise and are able to make a meaningful contribution. Rather, the Irish legislators are typified by the respondent who said that, "I try to speak on all the estimates." Not only does such a statement suggest a lack of expertise or specialized interest, it also leads one to wonder if this "interest" in policy is not primarily for the consumption of constituents.

Thus, the prediction appears to accord well with the realities of Irish politics. The apparent unity of Irish parties is born of lack of interest in policy, lack of substantial differences in the policy orientations of the parties, and the realization that parliamentary cohesion is necessary to the survival of cabinet government. As predicted by the theory of electorally determined parliamentary behavior, the matters of real importance to the deputies are constituency services, and on these matters deputies who must electioneer independently continue to act independently.

Italy

The central thrust of the argument with regard to Italian parties is summed up by Passigli's observation that "many an elected candidate has a double loyalty, one toward the party, the other toward . . . organizations that have made his electoral success possible or more assured."[32] For an Italian seeking nomination, the most important resource is the support of someone in the national party leadership who can press his claim to a favorable position on the party list.[33] Once nominated, the office seeker's principal electoral enemies are not candidates of other parties, but other candidates of his own party, with whom he must compete for the preference votes that determine which candidates will be elected. This means that each candidate must attempt to develop an independent campaign organization and access to resources beyond those provided by the party to all its candidates. Because of the way Italian society is structured, each of the resources needed to do this—organizational endorsements, newspaper support, funds, etc.—is controlled by the national leadership of a few organizations. For this reason, access to these leaders is tremendously important to a candidate, and a factional leader, by giving such access in return for support, can establish a powerful base within his party. Having done this, the faction leader is then in an even stronger position to act as broker between deputies and interests, and so to maintain his position.

At the same time, the electoral system of PR with large districts, especially when taken with the fact of categoric choice, encourages ideological competition among parties. The districts are far too large for personalism or localism to be dominant, yet the candidates are tied to factions that in turn are tied to organizations with specific policy preferences. As a result, the ideological style of competition tends to be important within the party as well. For these reasons, it was predicted that Italian parties would be composed of ideologically oriented factions based on the support of and access to special interest groups, mediated by factional leaders.

Italian political parties are distinguished from those in Britain and Ireland by at least three important characteristics. In the first place, Italian parties are far more ideological in approach than the other parties studied. This already has been demonstrated with regard to the campaign behavior of their candidates. In general, rather than simply differing in degree, each Italian party represents a distinctive view in a fundamentally unsettled debate as to the proper nature of Italian society. This ideological divergence is illustrated by the heavy moral, as opposed to pragmatic or opportunistic, tone of political debate over coalition formation in the parliament, and particularly by the trauma undergone by the DC over the inclusion of the PSI, and the DC's more recent internal dissension over the possibility of a *compromesso storico* with the Communists.[34] It is also reflected both in the kinds of strategic actions taken by the parliamentary parties and in the lines of argument used to justify these actions to the mass membership and extraparliamentary leaders.[35] Finally, the ideological orientation of Italian politicians has been documented in Putnam's sensitive comparison of the beliefs of British and Italian deputies.[36]

The second distinguishing characteristic of Italian political parties is the degree to which the entire range of interest groups common to all democratic industrial societies—labor unions, fraternal, patriotic, and women's groups, business and agricultural federations—is reproduced in clusters with clear party connections. Thus, there are three labor confederations, the Communist CGIL, the Catholic CISL, and the Social Democratic UIL; two organizations of small farmers, the Catholic Coltivatori Diretti and the Communist National Peasant's Alliance; Catholic Action's Union of Women and the Communist Union of Italian Women, and so forth. (Within each of the Communist-dominated organizations, there tends to be a subgroup of left wing Socialists; right wing Socialists frequently are found in the Social Democratic cluster of interest groups.)[37] These groups provide the basis for the third, and perhaps the most important, feature of Italian parties, their factionalism.

Although only the factions of the DC and PSI will be considered here, all Italian parties, including those that are ideologically opposed to factionalism (the Communists and the neo-fascist Italian Social Movement [MSI]), are divided between one or more ruling factions, or *correnti,* and a number of minority *correnti.*[38] These factions pervade virtually every level of party organization, with obvious identity within the parliamentary party delegations, organized slates of candidates for election to the parties' national committees, and clear patterns of allegiance among provincial secretaries.

Within the PSI, the primary basis of factionalism has been the ideological propriety of joining in coalition governments with bourgeois parties, allying with the Communists, or maintaining an autonomous position. The PSI is a moderate socialist party founded in 1892. Since then it has undergone a number of schisms resulting in the hiving off first of the maximalist Communist party and more recently the extremist Italian Socialist Party of Proletarian Unity (PSIUP) on the left, and the reformist Italian Social-Democratic Party (PSDI) on the right. Indeed, the PSI has existed in its current form only since the breakup of the PSI-PSDI Unificati after the 1968 general election. As always, the question was the proper stance of the party vis-à-vis the Communists on the one hand and the possibility of reforming the *centro-sinistra* government on the other.[39]

At the time of the 1968 general election, there were five basic *correnti* in the PSI-PSDI Unificati. At the extreme left, the Sinistra *corrente* under Riccardo Lombardi was opposed to any renewal of the center-left government with the DC and Republican Party (PRI). The two center-left *correnti,* Impegno Socialista under Antonio Giolitti and Riscossa Socialista led by Francesco De Martino, were prepared to enter a coalition government, but only if substantially greater concessions were made by the DC than had been the case under the previous coalition, while the center-right faction of Pietro Nenni and Giacomo Mancini, Autonomia Socialista, was prepared to enter the government with fewer conditions. The right wing faction, composed almost exclusively of Social Democrats (Rinnovamento Socialista with Mario Tanassi as leader) made the immediate resumption of the center-left formula the central point of its platform.[40] With breakoff of Rinnovamento to reinstitute the PSDI and the passage of time, by 1974 substantial realignment had taken place within the PSI, but with the same basic pattern remaining. On the left, three factions were represented on the party's central committee, Lombardi's Sinistra, a faction made up of members of the by then defunct PSIUP, and a small faction made up of left wing defectors from the DC, all of whom were former members of the Italian Association of Christian Workers (ACLI). Riscossa was dominant in the center along with a splinter faction that had broken away from it, the Bertoldiani. Finally on the right, Autonomia had split into a reduced Autonomia faction with Nenni as leader and Presenza Socialista under Mancini.

While there are clear ideological implications to factional membership within the PSI, personalism and the attractions of office, especially now that it has been experienced, are also important in determining factional alignments.[41] Thus, there is not a perfect correlation between left-right views on all issues and factional affiliation. Indeed, the Riscossa faction has had members with a quite broad range of views, attracted perhaps by the obvious personal benefits resulting from adherence to a clearly dominant faction.

There is a close relationship between policy preferences (particularly with regard to coalition formation and alliance with the Communists) and factional affiliation.[42] There are also relationships between interest group ties and factional affiliation, as was predicted. This is illustrated clearly by the finding of Spreafico and Cazzola with regard to union background. With CGIL dominated by the Communists, some right wing socialists are affiliated with the UIL instead. A perfect correlation was found between "leftness" of a faction and the proportion of its delegates to the 1968 PSI-PSDI National Congress belonging to the CGIL (ranging between 40 percent of the Sinistra delegates and none of the Rinnovamento delegates). A perfect correlation also was found between the "rightness" of a faction and the proportion of its delegates affiliated with the UIL (ranging between 24 percent of the Rinnovamento delegates and none of Sinistra).[43] This point also is illustrated by the fact that the defection of individuals from ACLI to the PSI occasioned the formation of a new faction.

The DC was not founded until after World War II, but is the clear successor of the prewar Popular party of Luigi Sturzo.[44] As a result of its primary basis as the Catholic party, the DC covers a wide range on the conventional left-right continuum. Some leaders, such as Carlo Donat-Cattin, philosophically are rooted in French social Catholicism and clearly are to the left of some Communists in terms of state intervention into the economy and redistribution of wealth to the working class. Some such leaders advocate a coalition government with the Communists, while other DC leaders find the MSI even more congenial as a coalition partner than the PSI. As befits the nation's largest party, the DC in 1971 had nine clearly identifiable factions in the Chamber of Deputies and the party *direzione* and each had its own press agency or periodical publication.[45] As was true of the Socialists, the DC was characterized by factional alignments that had clear ideological overtones; the factions of some DC leaders are obviously to the right (or left) of the factions of others. Even more than was the case with the PSI, however, the particular ideological position taken by the leaders seems to be determined by strategic considerations in a personal quest for power. Both the importance and the instability of the ideological positions taken by DC factional leaders are illustrated nicely by the case of Giulio Andreotti. In the 1950s and 1960s, he led a faction pressing for alliances with right wing parties; in 1970, his attempt to form a government failed because PSDI leaders feared that he was too leftist. In the early 1960s, Aldo Moro was considered to be to the right of Amintore Fanfani, then the leading spokesman on the left. Ten years later, Fanfani allied with Arnaldo Forlani in the Nuove Cronache faction, and Moro was considered to be well to their left.[46] In other words, while the electoral system presses for ideological competition among factions, neither factional membership nor the long-term strategy of factional leaders need be determined exclusively by ideological considerations. Instead, factional memberships based on common group ties and the provision of electorally important resources allow, and indeed encourage, factional leaders to compete for power within the party using ideology as a weapon, rather than as an end in itself.[47]

The relationship between factions of the DC and its various *parentela* groups has been observed on many occasions. Pasquino, for example, reports that the left wing factions consistently have been supported by CISL and ACLI, and on occasion by such state enterprises as the National Hydrocarbons Trust (ENI), while Giulio Andreotti's faction has been supported financially by Catholic Action.[48] A more exhaustive study reports that left and right wing factions have diametrically opposing interest group bases (tau = -1.0) while left and center factions also were found to differ greatly (tau = -0.60). In particular, 80 percent of the deputies of the left wing Rinnovamento faction were found to be leaders of CISL, while 80 percent of the Bonomiani were leaders of the Coltivatori Diretti. Every deputy with a business background was found to be a member of one of the center or right factions.[49] Other examples of interest group support for particular factions already have been cited.

The important distinction between Italian factions and the groups that are found in British parties is the degree to which the former are able to act in a manner unrestrained by and detrimental to party discipline. As Zariski observes, "Factionalism in Italian parties has greatly complicated the character of Italy's multiparty system. For what may appear to be a coalition composed of parties commanding a firm majority in Parliament may turn out to be a slender reed when one or more of the component parties contains a powerful faction that views the cabinet formula with hostility."[50] Perhaps as often as for any other reason, Italian cabinets fall because of the withdrawal, or threatened withdrawal, of support, not by a coalition partner of the DC but by one of the DC's own factional leaders. It is especially the ability of factional leaders to reach agreements cutting across party lines that underlines the validity of the predictions made in earlier chapters. Giorgio Amendola referred to such agreements in a speech to the PCI Central Committee, observing that, "In the past we have been able to unseat several governments, but always by reaching some agreement with a Christian Democratic faction (anti-Scelba, anti-Tambroni)."[51]

In terms of attitudes toward the job of deputy, Italians contrast almost completely with the Irish (see Table 6.1). Reflecting the policy orientation of Italian parties, over 80 percent reported that the most important part of a deputy's job is to participate in the formulation of policy. One-third of the responding Italian deputies reported that they felt themselves to be particularly expert in the field of industrial relations, probably reflecting the trade union backgrounds of many deputies of both parties. The other deputies gave responses scattered over the range of public policy.

Thus in the Italian case, the conformity is high between the deductively reached predictions and the observed reality. As was suggested in chapter 1, this is not surprising; it is well known that Italian parties are factionalized and that Irish deputies are oriented primarily toward patronage. What is significant is that these conclusions may be arrived at deductively, as well as by observation, and thus may be understood, as well as noted.

Addendum

The data on which the empirical chapters of this book, including this chapter, are based refer to the period of the 1950s through the early 1970s. Since that time, there have been two developments in the countries studied intensively that require brief comment here. The first is the emergence of open factional conflict between the supporters of Charles Haughey and those of George Colley to succeed Jack Lynch as the leader of the Fianna Fail party and as Taoiseach. Although there were some noticeable policy differences between the two candidates (Haughey is more conservative fiscally as well as being more avidly republican), the split appears to have been most markedly personal. It divided those who had received from the Lynch government special benefits, especially ministerial office, from the more patronage oriented "professional backbenchers" of the party. In keeping with the style of Irish politics predicted on the basis of the theory in chapter 2, and found to exist in the early 1970s on the basis of the data reported in chapters 4 through 6, Haughey since his victory has begun to turn the entire party and cabinet apparatus into a machine for the delivery of local services. While it is too early to say whether durable factions will emerge in the wake of this conflict, it is significant to note that in constituencies returning more than one Fianna Fail deputy, there was a definite tendency for the Fianna Fail delegation to be split in their support of the two candidates. All this is clearly consistent with the theory presented here.

The other development is the increased frequency and intensity of division within the British parties. This growth has been particularly evident in the extraparliamentary Labour party, but extends to the extraparliamentary Conservative party, and in a far milder and less organized form to the parliamentary parties as well. In terms of the theory presented here, the significant feature of these emerging divisions in the British parties is that they have been associated with a shift in the norms governing candidate selection. Where previously, as suggested above, local selectorates were concerned primarily with nominating a candidate who would serve as an effective spokesman for the party without regard to his personal views, they are acting increasingly as advocates of particular positions within the party rather than of the party as a whole. This has been especially true of the Labour left, and nowhere is the potential of this development for changing the character of the Labour party more evident than in the move debated in recent times to require a formal readoption (or nonreadoption) of sitting Labour MPs at each general election. Again, it is too early to tell what will happen, but were this trend to continue, with various constituency parties aligning strongly with particular unions, other organizations, or viewpoints, the competition within the party for nomination might take a more disruptive tone, and dependence on the continued support of such groups for renomination might become the basis of open factionalism in British parties, or more likely the stimulus for their disintegration. At the same time, the fate of the Independent Labour party after it disaffiliated from the Labour party in 1932 is still remembered by British politicians and serves as a powerful disincentive for those contemplating a break with their party.

7

Concluding Remarks

RETURNING to the three questions about party systems raised in chapter 1—number, orientation, and internal unity—the findings of this analysis regarding the link between electoral system and party system may be summarized quite briefly. As in earlier studies, the intensive analysis of three systems showed that the number of parties competing was related to the electoral formula and to the number of deputies returned from each district, with large-district PR systems tending to have the most parties and single-member plurality systems having the fewest. As in other recent analyses of the relationship between electoral systems and the number of parties, the simple formulation "the simple-majority [plurality] single ballot system favors the two party system"[1] was found to apply particularly at the district level rather than nationally. Extending beyond earlier work and looking at the number of different combinations of parties competing at the constituency level, it was found that single-member plurality systems, as exemplified by Great Britain, tend to have the most different local party systems, while large-district PR systems, exemplified by Italy, tend to have the fewest.

Both the extensive and the intensive analyses showed ideological style to be associated with proportional electoral formulae. With the ICPP data, significant correlations were observed between electoral formula and ideological style, as indicated by issue extremism, consistency, and appeal to a codified party doctrine. These correlations by themselves cannot support a "sociological law," but since the indirect measures available are of clearly limited validity and other factors of obvious importance are uncontrolled, overwhelming correlations could not reasonably be expected. Yet, those correlations that were observed, especially with regard to extremism and doctrinism, were quite strong. Further support for the hypothesis was gleaned from the intensive analysis, with the British, Irish, and Italian parties clearly behaving as expected.

One further point arising in this part of the intensive analysis deserves repetition here. While it was suggested that PR systems are associated with more highly nationalized electoral effects, both in terms of explained variance in election returns and in terms of common campaign emphasis, this does not necessarily mean greater emphasis on "national" issues. Rather, candidates in plurality systems may adapt to their varied competitive environments by stressing local issues, as in Ireland, *or* by stressing a few national issues that may vary from constituency to constituency, as in Britain. In either case, electoral nationalization will be reduced. The current theory does not allow a prediction of which adaptation is most likely in any given system, although a few important variables can be suggested that might be relevant, among them centralization of policy making and administration or level of political and cultural development.

Ideology is only one way in which a concern with issues might be manifested, so that nonideological parties nonetheless may show high levels of policy orientation. In particular, evidence was presented suggesting that this party characteristic is significantly conditioned by the magnitude of districts and the nature of choice—whether ordinal or categoric. Based on the number of issues on which a party's position could be determined clearly, the incidence of ideological and policy debate and disagreement among party leaders, and the importance of purposive incentives in mobilizing party militants, the extensive analysis showed the nature of choice to be clearly related to issue orientation. The relationship between issue orientation and district magnitude was somewhat weaker, but still generally as expected. Again strong support for the hypotheses was found in the three-country intensive analysis, although here the perfect correlation of district magnitude and nature of choice prevented differentiation of these factors.

Finally, it was suggested that internal disunity tends to be the result of electoral competition within the party. The most direct way for this to come about is through the existence of an intraparty preference vote. The ICPP parties competing in systems with preferential voting were shown to be more likely to have diffused leadership, although not more likely than others to be actually factionalized. The particular form and arena in which this disunity is manifested depends on the distribution of mobilizable resources and the orientation of the political system. Where resources are diffused so that each candidate must build his own support coalition in order to compete for preference votes, the resulting party is likely to be fractionalized. On the other hand, centralization of control over resources increases the likelihood of factionalism, with faction leaders serving a brokerage function between groups of individual candidates and their common supporters. These conclusions are supported clearly by the cases of Britain and Italy, and by the Irish example as well once an additional complicating factor is taken into account. In all parliamentary systems, there is a pressure toward unity imposed by the desire to achieve or retain office. When policy questions are of virtually no interest to either voters or politicians, this pressure for unity is likely to override the pressure for disunity brought about by the electoral system—but only in the policy area. In fields of greater importance (in the Irish case this was constituency patronage), the expected pattern of disunity prevails, heightened by the additional intraparty competition for nomination that the de facto requirement of local connections engenders.

While the substance of these findings may be stated simply, their significance is more far-reaching. In particular, this analysis has implications both for the understanding of elite political behavior and for the theory of democratic political institutions. Consideration of these problems returns one to the broad questions implicit to chapter 1: how are party systems to be explained, and how do electoral systems, through their impact on parties, shape the quality of democracy found in a country?

Many of the empirical conclusions of this study repeat the findings and suggestions of earlier studies. But there is a difference between knowing something to be so and understanding why. Causation ultimately is not an empirical, but a philosophical, phenomenon. It is imputed rather than shown; argued for rather than proven. This means that explanations must be grounded on assumptions that are more metaphysical than real, and thus must be judged by their utility for understanding, rather than by their "accuracy." The assumptions that make explanation possible are those that define a paradigm, and one purpose of this analysis has been to demonstrate the utility of one particular paradigm—the rationalist or economic paradigm —for understanding the political behavior of elites.

In this respect, the important factor is not the substance of the empirical findings, but rather the method by which the hypotheses tested were derived. This study started with two simple assumptions, that politicians are motivated primarily by a desire to win elections and that they pursue this goal as if acting rationally. From these assumptions were deduced the characteristics of party systems to be expected on the basis of differing electoral systems. That these conclusions could be deduced from a few simple assumptions, and that not only the final conclusions, but many of the intermediate predictions that led to them as well, could be verified empirically, lends important support to the argument as an explanation. Moreover, this support is not limited to the explanation of systemic differences among party systems as developed here. Rather, the success of this explanation offers evidence of the general utility of the rationalistic approach in explaining elite political behavior.

Elite behavior has been explained in a variety of different ways. For some, sociological variables have appeared most important. The class backgrounds of politicians and the relative strengths of the social classes and other groups in society are seen to determine the direction of politics and the operation of political institutions.[2] For others, psychological factors appear to play the primary role. Thus system level differences might be explained in terms of differing child rearing patterns or family structures, while appeal might be made to the individual childhood experiences of politicians in order to explain variations within a single system.[3]

The rationalistic paradigm is an alternative to these types of explanation, but this does not mean it suggests that the variables with which other explanations are concerned are irrelevant to politics. Instead, the rationalistic paradigm offers a rationale whereby a variety of specific influences may be integrated into a more general theory. An example from the present theory is the way in which factionalism or fractionalization was suggested to depend on the distribution of control over political resources. Here, a sociological variable plays a prominent role, but not because of its own explanatory power. Rather, it is the influence of this situational variable on the rational choices of individuals that makes it appear important. Likewise, the distribution of people and other political resources within society is important because it opens or forecloses different strategies in the pursuit of goals and makes their success more or less likely. Other variables affecting the way in which political or personal objectives may be pursued effectively can be integrated into a rationalistic theory in the same manner.

In explaining system level differences in party structure, it has been fruitful to assume that all politicians single-mindedly pursue the single goal of reelection. This is obviously an oversimplification and it limits the ability of the deductively derived theory to explain all the nuances of party structure. Nonetheless, for explaining the similarities within a single system and the differences among systems, it is an oversimplification with considerable attraction. To go farther in explaining detailed differences within systems requires a more detailed and variegated basis for inference. In part, differences in behavior may be explained with reference to differences in the situations of various actors. Behavioral differences also may be explained by differences in the goals these actors pursue. Here the rationalistic paradigm allows the explicit introduction of psychological and ideological variables, as well as those concerning sociological influences. Representatives of distinct classes may behave differently because their objective situations or life experiences give them different interests to pursue. Distinct psychological types may have different internal needs that lead to different external behavior patterns. Clearly, the policy goals pursued by politicians will vary with their ideological commitments, thus leading to differences in behavior. As with situational variables, the use of the rationalistic paradigm not only gives clues to factors that are likely to be correlated with the behavior explained, but also suggests how these correlations fit into an understandable causal pattern.

Of course, all this depends on one's ability to make plausible assumptions about the goals of actors, without which one returns to the dilemma of being able only to say, "He did what he did because he wanted to." It is for this reason that the rationalistic paradigm has proven more useful in explaining the behavior of politicians than that of average citizens. For example, while it is unrealistic to assume that candidates for office are motivated exclusively by a desire for victory, it is entirely reasonable to assume that they are so motivated to a very large degree. On the other hand, while citizens may be motivated in some measure by a desire to influence the outcome of an election with their individual votes, to assume that this is an important influence leads to the conclusion that rational citizens will not vote at all.[4] Not only are the stakes higher for candidates than for voters; candidates' actions are also more likely to have an effect. Further, because they are less numerous, elite actors may be studied more intensively, so that assumptions about differing motivations need not have such a strong *post hoc* flavor.[5] Where one can make reasonable simplifying assumptions regarding motivation, the rationalistic approach may be of significant use. With sufficient data, one might be able to do this even for members of the mass public with their infinitely varying political goals, interests, and backgrounds.[6] For the present, this is likely to be possible only for elites for whom important goals like the acquisition and retention of office and power can be identified.

If the conclusions of this study are correct concerning the linkages between electoral systems and party systems, then this work also has significant implications for democratic theory and for the reform of democratic institutions. Naturally, the evaluation of any given electoral or party system depends on one's definition of, and taste for, democracy, a problem beyond the scope of this work. But, if electoral and party systems are causally tied to one another, it makes little sense to discuss possible modifications of one in isolation from the other, regardless of one's specific preferences concerning democracy.

Many students of democracy have been concerned with the internal democracy of parties.[7] For them, competition among parties is not sufficient for true democracy. Thus, while recognizing the need for leadership if representative assemblies are not to be mere debating societies, Frank Goodnow warns that, "A popular representative form of government with an autocratic party organization controlled by an oligarchy or a party despot may not result in as really a popular political system, i.e., may not permit of as ready an expression of the popular or state will, as a less popular form of government combined with a less autocratic form of party organization."[8] As a result, Goodnow argues that democracy is best served, given the propensity of unrestrained leaders to act despotically, if candidates are selected in primaries in which all of the party's supporters may vote.[9] Similarly, John Stuart Mill proposed as the best way to further his ideal of representative government, an electoral system involving an intraparty choice similar to that used in Ireland.[10] Preferential voting has been defended in PR systems as a means of allowing greater popular involvement in the selection of leadership, and thus increasing the quality of democracy.

This study suggests, however, that these conclusions are based on unrealistic hopes for intraparty democracy. The genius of mass party democracy as developed in the twentieth century is that it permits average citizens to organize, and so to make up with numbers for what they lack in individual wealth and influence. The intraparty preference vote tends to undo this, however, by making politicians dependent on powerful patrons for the resources necessary for electoral competition *within* the party. It is logically possible that factions might develop akin to mass parties within the party—an eventuality with its own theoretical problems. In fact, party factions tend to be much more like the caucus parties of the early nineteenth century, in which popular control was far more dubious. Fractionalized parties simply present the intraparty analog of nonparty democracy with the attendant problems mentioned in chapter 1. Thus, quite contrary to Goodnow's belief, an institutional attempt to impose popular control within political parties may well be self-defeating. Indeed, by preventing the "group of working politicians" (who have a vital self-interest in satisfying the entire body of party supporters) from choosing candidates and strategies that will maximize their party's electoral chances,[11] and by encouraging party disintegration, an attempt at popular control actually may be pernicious.

Another common concern among democratic theorists is with the accuracy of representation. Although mirroring the distribution of opinions in society is only one aspect of representation,[12] it is one given considerable attention by many, especially by those who in this sense are underrepresented. Single-member plurality election naturally leaves large numbers of people unrepresented in the sense that no candidate of the parties they supported was elected from their constituencies. Even taking the broader view that an individual is represented if someone who agrees with her is elected from some other district and so is able to speak for her point of view in the parliament,[13] the various shades of opinion in society are hardly likely to be represented in fair proportion to their actual support.[14] In part, the logic of single-member plurality election forces major parties to reach compromises and accommodations with minorities before elections, but many other minorities are simply left unrepresented.

One frequent response to these problems is support of PR. This naturally tends to increase the number of parties represented in the parliament, thus making single-party majorities less likely (although it should be recognized that the pressure for the adoption of PR usually has been strongest only after a multiparty system already has been established). As a result, many of the accommodations reached before the election in two-party plurality systems must be reached in the legislature instead.[15] This may be defended reasonably as desirable, since in the legislature various groups are represented more fairly. It may also be a necessity, if societal cleavages are so deep as to prevent accommodation at the mass level.[16] Further, unless there are in fact not only "two sides to every issue,"[17] but only two complexes of sides for all issues,[18] no one majority accurately can reflect the popular will on all issues; multiparty PR systems allow different coalitions to form for different policy questions.

The problem is that PR not only increases the fairness of representation, but also induces a chance in the style of parties and in the nature of the competition among them. The move to PR produces pressure toward ideology while discouraging convergence of parties, which instead are led to maximize the importance of their differences. The result is that while PR makes compromises among parties in the parliament more necessary, it also makes them more difficult to achieve. Parties that have taken ideological positions find pragmatic compromises difficult to make. Further, the most likely coalition partners in the legislature are the parties in the most direct electoral competition, a situation hardly calculated to promote amicable cooperation. Moreover, if the distribution of seats is such as to inhibit turnover in office, as is the case in Italy, irresponsibility by those permanently excluded from office, and paralytic conservatism by those permanently in office, are likely results. Shifting alliances may prevent any group of politicians from remaining in power long enough to be interested in or capable of long-term planning. Thus, the attempt to improve the quality of democracy by improving the accuracy of representation carries with it the risk of instability or immobilism in the government. While the popular will may be expressed accurately, there may be no one with the capacity to carry that will into effect.

As well as influencing the "fairness" with which parties are represented, the choice between PR and plurality electoral systems also affects the very basis and character of representation itself. In PR systems, parties and by extension the ideological groups for which they stand, are represented. Citizens are represented by deputies of their parties from their districts, but the deputies' primary allegiance is to party rather than to locality. While there may be a few district interests that cut across party lines and produce cooperation among deputies from different parties but from the same area, these are in contradiction to the basic logic of PR. Ordinarily, the PR deputy does not represent the district as a whole, but only his party's supporters within it. In contrast, in plurality systems, and especially in single-member plurality systems, the deputy's role as representative of a particular area is emphasized. The member is expected to speak for the district and for the personal interests of all his constituents, not just those of his own party. Thus single-member plurality systems lay stress on personalistic representation; each citizen has "her" deputy. In PR systems, groups are represented by parties.[19] The single-member plurality system encourages compromise and moderation at least at the district level; PR systems discourage them.

Put in its most favorable light, a plurality system would appear to moderate conflict and aid in the coalition building process whose success is vital to the peaceful and effective solution of social problems, while increasing the feeling in each citizen that she is represented personally in government. But as the arguments developed here suggest, these coalitions, which in any case are built locally rather than at the national level, are frequently forged by the simple expedient of ignoring policy questions while emphasizing particularistic interests, and the personal voice the citizen feels she has is most often used to press for favorable treatment of personal problems. Since the basis of representation is residence rather than interest or policy preference, legislators may become reluctant to deal with tendentious issues, for fear that any action will cost votes; having avoided policy positions as candidates, they try to avoid them as deputies. Although plurality systems make compromise more possible by encouraging moderation, they discourage dealing with difficult problems at all. In plurality systems, providing local benefits, even at a significant cost to the national interest, frequently undermines the capacity of the government to take effective action. If the purpose of representation is to ensure that each area gets its share of the pie, this is not a serious problem. But if representation is to provide a mechanism whereby the national interest may be found and acted upon, the conservatism inherent in an approach based on local service may be of greater concern.

Roughly the same problem arises when one considers the distinction between ordinal and categoric choice. An ordinal choice may be defended in two ways, each of which appears to sow the seeds of its own contradiction. First, recognizing that there will not be unanimity within any party on all policy questions, the ordinal choice allows voters to pick and choose among all the available candidates. The immediate result might be more accurate representation,[20] and the longer-term result might be to encourage the parties to nominate more candidates of a particularly popular persuasion. In fact, however, the effect more often is to blur the distinctions among both candidates and parties. As the differences among candidates shrink, the voter has a narrowed range of choice, and as these differences are played down by the candidates, she becomes less able to choose meaningfully. Thus the quality of representation, at least in terms of the important policy questions of the day, is likely to suffer instead of being improved.

Second, the ordinal choice may be defended as giving greater flexibility to the voter, allowing a more complex set of preferences to be expressed. This increased freedom may appear desirable, but actually it is self-defeating, for the increased freedom in the casting of votes undermines the power of the votes cast. In representative democracies, citizens can express their will only by choosing parties committed to specific actions or philosophies, and then they must rely on those parties to carry their promises into effect. The legitimate authority of parties winning elections comes precisely from the fact that they have been endorsed by the voters. An ordinal choice, however, both discourages parties from taking clear stands and undermines the clarity with which the winners may claim to have popular support. While categoric choice limits the voter's ability to express complex preferences and differing shades of opinion, it increases the clarity and therefore the power of the preferences expressed. Again, the less "democratic" institution may well produce the more "democratic" result.

These are only a few of the limitations imposed on the possible reform of democratic institutions by the fact that party systems and electoral systems are tied to one another through the self-interest of politicians. No doubt, a more comprehensive analysis would uncover more limitations. These examples are adequate, however, to illustrate the distinction between theoretically desirable and practically efficacious reforms. There appear to be limits to the perfectability of political institutions, limits imposed by the humanity of those who operate them. Politicians are neither anonymous cogs with no independent wills in the machinery of government, nor self-denying idealists prepared to sacrifice their personal interests and identities to promote the efficient operation of a theoretically defined system of government. Instead, they are people with both public and private goals. One great virtue of the rationalistic paradigm is to underscore the importance of private goals, without consideration of which reform efforts are likely to produce many unforeseen, and possibly undesirable, results.[21]

If this analysis suggests severe limitations on the desirability of electoral system reform, what of the possibility or likelihood of reforms? Naturally minor adjustments are to be expected, but major changes should be unlikely. Electoral laws must be changed by politicians who have been successful under the current system.[22] Successful politicians have developed party organizations appropriate to those systems. Clearly then, if reforms are to occur, politicians must be convinced to rise above their self-interest, to change the rules of a game that they are winning. This is something that seems likely only when, as in France after the Second World War or during the Algerian crisis, the nation seems on the verge of collapse.

Sampling

SAMPLING for the questionnaires used in this study was based on constituency. In all three countries, stratified random samples of constituencies, weighted according to the number of deputies returned, were drawn. The sampling strata were regions. In Great Britain, the regions were London, England other than London, Scotland, and Wales; Northern Ireland was excluded. In Eire, the sampling strata were the four historic provinces of Ireland plus the borough of Dublin. The Italian strata were the North of Italy, the Center, and the Mezzogiorno, with Sicily, Sardegna, the Valle d'Aosta, and Trieste eliminated.

The total British sample size was sixty constituencies. An attempt was made to send questionnaires to (or obtain interviews with) the candidates and agents of both major parties at the time of the 1970 general election in each constituency selected. (While either a Labour or a Conservative candidate was elected from each of the sampled constituencies, in some cases the candidate of the other major party finished third.) Questionnaires for the defeated candidates and agents were sent to the constituency party headquarters, and in some cases were returned with the notation that the person to whom they were addressed had left the constituency with no forwarding address. This reduced the original sample of 240 individuals to 196. Eventually 110 interviews or completed questionnaires were obtained for an overall response rate of 56 percent of the reduced sample.

The Irish sample consisted of seven constituencies, including twenty-four deputies of Fianna Fail and Fine Gael, or about one-fifth of the total, as opposed to just under one-tenth in Britain. An attempt was made to interview personally all deputies of the two parties elected from these constituencies. Questionnaires were sent to the defeated candidates of the two parties at the addresses listed on their nominating forms. Twenty such questionnaires were sent. Since the parties refused to provide the names and addresses of local party officials, each responding deputy and candidate was asked to supply the name and address of one branch secretary from his own constituency party. In all, fourteen did so, yeilding a total potential sample of fifty-eight. Of these, twenty-eight responded, giving a total response rate of 48 percent.

There were nine constituencies in the Italian sample. Questionnaires were sent to all PSI deputies, representing just under one-third of the total number of PSI members of the Chamber of Deputies, and to an equal number of DC deputies randomly selected from the same constituencies with sampling based on factional affiliation. Questionnaires also were sent to one defeated candidate (when an address could be obtained) and one federation secretary of each party in each constituency. In all, seventy-eight questionnaires were sent. Due to the chaotic state of the Italian postal service at the time of this research, there is no way of telling how many of these questionnaires actually were delivered, but twenty-four completed forms eventually were received, for a response rate of 31 percent of the total sample.

In each case, the response rate was approximately constant across parties and regions, and in each case the response rate was lowest for defeated candidates and highest among elected deputies. There is a slight underrepresentation of ministers and front bench opposition spokesmen in all three countries (especially among British ministers), but in general a surprisingly large number of prominent people responded. While the response rates are far from high and the samples were not large, the overall representativeness of the samples coupled with the overwhelming differences observed between countries appears to compensate for this. As has been observed, these differences were shown to be statistically significant with tests designed to be used with samples of this size drawn from infinite populations, and thus there seems to be no reason to doubt the validity of the findings reported here on the grounds of sampling bias.

Questionnaire

ALTOGETHER, nine forms of the questionnaire used in this study were prepared, matched to the respondent's status (deputy, defeated candidate, or party official) and nationality. The questions reproduced below are those asked in Ireland. When asked of British respondents, identical wording was used except that *House of Commons* or *House* was substituted for *Dail* and *MP* was substituted for *TD;* in the Italian translation, the equivalent of *TD* was *Deputato* and the equivalent of *Dail* was *Camera dei Deputati.* Only those questions from which data reported in the text were taken are reproduced. Questions marked with an asterisk (*) were not asked in Britain; those marked with a dagger (†) were not asked in Italy; those marked with a number sign (#) were asked only in Italy. A variety of personal questions—age, sex, party, career history—also were asked but are not reproduced here.

Asked of Candidates and Deputies Only

At the time of the campaign, did you live in the constituency in which you stood in the last general election, and if so, for how long have you lived there?

——I did not live in the constituency.

——I have lived in the constituency only since my adoption as a candidate for the Dail.

——I lived in the constituency for less than 2 years before my adoption as a candidate for the Dail.

——I lived in the constituency for between 2 years and 10 years before my adoption as a candidate for the Dail.

——I had lived in the constituency for longer than 10 years when I was adopted as a candidate for the Dail.

In what year were you first selected as a candidate for the Dail in this constituency (or in the constituency which encompassed nearly the same area under a previous division of seats)?

———

If you were first selected as a candidate in some other constituency, please list below the constituencies in which you have been a candidate and the elections in which you stood for those constituencies.

Constituency   Elections

_____   _____

_____   _____

Did you solicit the support of any national or local party leaders before the constituency selection meetings in your effort to secure adoption as a candidate?
——I solicited the support of both national and local leaders.
——I solicited the support of national leaders only.
——I solicited the support of local leaders only.
——I did not solicit the support of any party leaders before the constituency selection meetings.

Would you say that it was originally your idea that you become a candidate for the Dail or did someone else suggest it to you?
——Becoming a candidate was my own idea.
——Becoming a candidate was suggested by a relative or a personal friend.
——Becoming a candidate was suggested by a local party leader.
——Becoming a candidate was suggested by a national party leader.
——Becoming a candidate was suggested by some other person. (Please specify ——)

*How much did your personal campaign cost in the last general election?
——

Would you say that your own campaign focused on national or local issues?
—— National Issues   ——Local Issues

What specific issues did you emphasize in your campaign?
_____

Is there any area of governmental policy in which you feel yourself particularly qualified to contribute, and if so what area is that?
_____
——Please tick this space if there is no area of policy in which you feel particularly qualified.

Asked of Party Officials Only

When the candidates who represented your party in this constituency at the last general election were first selected, what TDs or national party leaders supported their adoption.
_____   _____

In general, what effect did their support have on the adoption of the candidates they backed?
——Aided them a great deal.
——Aided them somewhat.
——Made no difference at all.
——Hurt them somewhat.
——Hurt them a great deal.

At that time, did any of the candidates finally adopted contact you before the formal selection meetings to try to solicit your support?
——Yes   ——No

Did any of the candidates who were not adopted contact you?
——Yes   ——No

If any of the candidates for adoption did anything in addition to attending selection meetings to try to secure adoption as one of your party's candidates, what did they do and would you say that it helped them or hurt them?

_____

Asked of All Respondents (Wording Varied with Office)

Could you rank the following in order of their importance to your adoption as candidate, giving *1* to the one which *you* consider to have been most important, *2* to the second most important, *3* to the third most important, *4* to the fourth most important, and so forth for each item listed.
——Personal contacts within the constituency.
——Endorsements of national party leaders.
——Endorsements of local party leaders.
——Residence within the constituency.
——Previous political experience or achievements.
——Trade union or other group backing.
——Your personality.
——Your personal political views.

Thinking now of the last general election, could you rank each of the following as "Very Important" (VI), "Important" (IM), "Not Very Important" (NVI), or "Irrelevant" (IR) in determining the outcome in your constituency?

	VI	IM	NVI	IR
National issues	——	——	——	——
Local issues	——	——	——	——
National leaders	——	——	——	——
Local leaders	——	——	——	——

*Could you rate the importance of each of the following in determining the order in which voters prefer the candidates of a single party in your constituency?

	VI	IM	NVI	IR
Candidates' policy views	——	——	——	——
Candidates' places of residence	——	——	——	——
Candidates' political experience	——	——	——	——
Endorsements of national leaders	——	——	——	——
Endorsements of local leaders	——	——	——	——
Differences in the degree to which candidates are known	——	——	——	——
# *Corrente*	——	——	——	——

Could you rate the importance of each of the following in influencing voters in your constituency?

	VI	IM	NVI	IR
Television and radio campaigns	——	———	———	——
National newspaper endorsements	——	———	———	——
Local newspaper endorsements	——	———	———	——
National newspaper advertising	——	———	———	——
Local newspaper advertising	——	———	———	——
Speeches by national leaders	——	———	———	——
Speeches by local leaders	——	———	———	——
+ Personal canvassing	——	———	———	——

About how much would you estimate was spent by your party and its candidates, both before and during the formal campaign period, in this constituency in the last general election?

——$0–$250   ——$1,250–$2,500   —— $6,250–$12,500
——$250–$625   ——$2,500–$3,750   —— $12,500–$25,000
——$625–$1,250   ——$3,750–$6,250   —— $25,000 or more

(Asked in local currency.)

Did any national party leaders campaign in your constituency, and if so, who were they [and did they campaign for you personally, for some other candidate of your party personally, or for all the candidates of your party]? (Bracketed portion not asked in Britain.)

	For Me Only	For Another Candidate	For All Candidates
_____	——	——	——
_____	——	——	——
_____	——	——	——

About how many people were actively involved in your campaign in the last general election?

_____

How were these people primarily recruited?
——From outside the constituency.
——By the constituency party
——By local branches throughout the constituency.
——As individual volunteers from all over the constituency.
——By local branches only in your area of the constituency.
——As individual volunteers from only your area in the constituency.
——By organized groups outside the party.

What do you think is the single most important part of a TD's job?

_____

_____

Are there any groups within the party that tend to stick together behind a particular leader?

——Yes   ——No

Notes

Chapter 1

1. For example, see Hans Kelsen, *La Democratie: Sa Nature, Sa Valeur*, trans. Charles Eisenmann (Paris: Recueil Sirey, 1932), p. 19; E. E. Schattschneider, *Party Government* (New York: Rinehart and Winston, 1942), p. 1; Graham Wallas, *Human Nature in Politics* (New York: A. A. Knopf, 1931), p. 103; V. O. Key, Jr., *Politics, Parties, and Pressure Groups* (New York: Alfred A. Knopf, 1964), p. 9.

2. See Giovanni Sartori, *Democratic Theory* (Detroit: Wayne State University Press, 1962), especially pt. II; Joseph Schumpeter, *Capitalism, Socialism, and Democracy* (New York: Harper, 1950), p. 242.

3. See the American Political Science Association report, *Toward a More Responsible Two Party System* (New York: Rinehart, 1950).

4. Asa Briggs, *The Making of Modern Britain* (New York: Harper and Row, 1965), chap. 10.

5. Giovanni Sartori, "European Political Parties: The Case of Polarized Pluralism," in Joseph LaPalombara and Myron Weiner, eds., *Political Parties and Political Development* (Princeton: Princeton University Press, 1966), pp. 137–76; see also, P. Allum, *Italy— Republic Without Government?* (New York: W. W. Norton, 1973).

6. Gerhard Loewenberg, "The Remarking of the German Party System," in Mattei Dogan and Richard Rose, eds., *European Politics* (Boston: Little, Brown, 1971), pp. 259–79.

7. See Austin Ranney, *The Doctrine of Responsible Party Government* (Urbana: University of Illinois Press, 1962).

8. Anthony Downs, *An Economic Theory of Democracy* (New York: Harper and Row, 1957), chap. 9.

9. See Robert A. Dahl, *A Preface to Democratic Theory* (Chicago: University of Chicago Press, 1956), chap. 5.

10. See A. J. Milnor, *Elections and Political Stability* (Boston: Little, Brown, 1969), pp. 188–89.

11. David R. Mayhew, "Congressional Representation: Theory and Practice in Drawing the Districts," in Nelson W. Polsby, ed., *Reapportionment in the 1970s* (Berkeley: University of California Press, 1971), p. 272.

12. For some notes on the definition of party, see Sigmund Neumann, "Toward a Comparative Study of Political Parties," in his *Modern Political Parties* (Chicago: University of Chicago Press, 1958), pp. 395–96; Leon D. Epstein, *Political Parties in Western Democracies* (New York: Praeger, 1967), pp. 9–14; Seymour Martin Lipset and Stein Rokkan, *Party Systems and Voter Alignments* (New York: Free Press, 1967), pp. 3–4.

13. See Richard Rose, "Parties, Factions, and Tendencies in Britain," *Political Studies* 12 (February 1964): 33–46; Raphael Zariski, "Party Factions and Comparative Politics: Some Preliminary Observations," *Midwest Journal of Political Science* 4 (February 1960): 32–33; V. O. Key, Jr., *Southern Politics* (New York: Alfred A. Knopf, 1949), pp. 15–18.

14. Indeed, these are the examples chosen by Sartori to illustrate factions within parties. Giovanni Sartori, *Parties and Party Systems* (Cambridge: Cambridge University Press, 1976), pp.88–93.

15. Michael Leiserson, "Factions and Coalitions in One-Party Japan," *American Political Science Review* 63 (September 1968): 770–87.

16. Austin Ranney, *Pathways to Parliament* (Madison: University of Wisconsin Press, 1965), p. 10.

17. Ranney's conclusion may be a bit overstated, in that there is almost certainly a two-way process of "anticipated reactions" operating between national and local arms of the party. However, as the example of Reg Prentice shows, in cases of conflict it still appears that the local party will have its way. Recent events also suggest that a member disowned by the local party may be able to win reelection as an Independent. See Austin Ranney, "Selecting the Candidates," in Howard R. Penniman, ed., *Britain at the Polls* (Washington: American Enterprise Institute for Public Policy Research, 1975), pp. 33–60; Anthony King, "The MPs' New Freedom," *New Society,* 14 March 1974, 639–40.

18. Aneurin Bevan, quoted in Richard H. S. Crossman, *The Myths of Cabinet Government* (Cambridge, Mass.: Harvard University Press, 1972), p. 32.

19. Epstein, *Political Parties,* pp. 318–32; idem, "Cohesion in British Parliamentary Parties," *American Political Science Review* 50 (June 1956): 360–77.

20. Key, *Politics, Parties, and Pressure Groups,* p. 342.

21. The direct primary apparently is used quite vigorously in Costa Rica.

22. Nathaniel B. Thayer, *How the Conservatives Rule Japan* (Princeton: Princeton University Press, 1969), chap. 2. Similar arguments and additional evidence may be found in Haruhiro Fukui, *Party In Power* (Canberra: Australian National University Press, 1970), esp. chaps. 5,6. Factionalism in the Japanese left is discussed in Allan B. Cole, George O. Totten, and Cecil H. Uyehara, *Socialist Parties in Postwar Japan* (New Haven: Yale University Press, 1966), chap. 9.

23. See Ardath W. Burks, *The Government of Japan* (New York: Thomas Crowell, 1961), pp. 113–14 for a description of the Japanese electoral law.

24. Raphael Zariski, *Italy: The Politics of Uneven Development* (Hinsdale, Ill.: Dryden Press, 1972), p. 195.

25. Donald T. Campbell, "'Degrees of Freedom' and the Case Study," *Comparative Political Studies* 8 (July 1975): 178–93.

26. Brian Barry, *Sociologists, Economists, and Democracy* (London: Collier-Macmillan, 1970), pp. 3–6; Robert T. Holt and John M. Richardson, Jr., "Competing Paradigms in Comparative Politics," in Robert T. Holt and John E. Turner, eds., *The Methodology of Comparative Research* (New York: Free Press, 1970), pp. 21–72.

27. On this problem, see Mancur Olson, Jr., *The Logic of Collective Action* (New York: Schocken, 1965).

28. Downs, *Economic Theory of Democracy,* esp. pt. III; William H. Riker and Peter C. Ordeshook, *An Introduction to Positive Political Theory* (Englewood Cliffs, N.J.: Prentice-Hall, 1973), pp. 187–88, 191–92.

29. See the forward to Downs, *Economic Theory of Democracy,* by Stanley Kelley, Jr.

30. David Mayhew makes this argument in the particular case of the U.S. Congress in *Congress: The Electoral Connection* (New Haven: Yale University Press, 1974). See also, Lawrence C. Dodd, "Congress and the Quest for Power," in Lawrence C. Dodd and Bruce I. Oppenheimer, eds., *Congress Reconsidered* (New York: Praeger, 1977), pp. 269–307.

31. Abraham Kaplan, *The Conduct of Inquiry: Methodology for Behavioral Science* (San Francisco: Chandler, 1964), esp. chaps. 7, 8.

32. Indeed, a full analysis probably would include such devices as rational responses to the cost of information.

33. Ronald Rogowski is making a similar argument when he observes that "the corner grocer seldom carries out the computations by which the professor of microeconomics tries to

predict his behavior" (*Rational Legitimacy* [Princeton: Princeton University Press, 1974], p. 32).

34. The focus on electoral systems as determiners of political behavior owes much to the work of Maurice Duverger. See especially, "The Influence of Electoral Systems on Political Life," *International Social Science Bulletin* 3 (Summer 1951): 342–70.

35. Downs, *Economic Theory of Democracy,* p. 21.

36. See Fred N. Kerlinger and Elazar J. Pedhazur, *Multiple Regression in Behavioral Research* (New York: Holt, Rinehart and Winston, 1973), pp. 4–5, for a particularly strong statement of this view.

37. This example is from Kerlinger and Pedhazur, *Multiple Regression,* p. 16.

38. This is only true for the intermediate conclusions that one's theory suggests are important, in this case, those relating to candidates' behavior but not their thought processes. To take a mundane example, to the hobbyist, a model train must conform to reality in appearance, although not in mass or inertial characteristics. In contrast, for the designer of signal systems using mathematical models, inertial characteristics are crucial while appearance is of no consequence. Again, no model simpler than reality can conform to reality in all respects.

39. William H. Riker, *The Theory of Political Coalitions* (New Haven: Yale University Press, 1962).

40. See Kenneth Janda, "A Worldwide Study of Political Parties," in Benjamin Mittman and Lorraine Borman, eds., *Personalized Data Base Systems* (New York: John Wiley and Sons, 1975), pp. 129–37; idem, "The Status of the International Comparative Political Parties Project," *International Studies Newsletter* (Winter 1973): 49–52.

Chapter 2

1. For a discussion of this type of theory, see Donald E. Stokes, "Spatial Models of Party Competition," in Angus Campbell et al., *Elections and the Political Order* (New York: John Wiley and Sons, 1966), pp. 161–79. See also, William H. Riker and Peter C. Ordeshook, *An Introduction to Positive Political Theory* (Englewood Cliffs, N.J.: Prentice-Hall, 1973), chaps. 11, 12.

2. This is not to say the parties do not, in reality, change their platforms during campaigns, only that the selection of a platform and possible modifications of it are beyond the scope of the present theory.

3. This assumption is particularly reasonable in the context of parliamentary democracy where legislative party cohesion in voting may be expected, both theoretically and empirically, to be quite high.

4. For a description of the "city-block" metric, see Douglas W. Rae and Michael Taylor, "Decision Rules and Policy Outcomes," *British Journal of Political Science* 1 (January 1971): 71–90. Empirical support for the assumption that voters do think this way may be found in many places, but Giacomo Sani, "A Test of the Least Distance Model of Voting Choice: Italy, 1972," *Comparative Political Studies* 7 (July 1974): 193–208 is particularly relevant.

5. For example, even with a potential fine of almost $50 for abstention, turnout in Australian elections is only about 95 percent. Kevin P. Phillips and Paul H. Blackman, *Electoral Reform and Voter Participation* (Washington: American Enterprise Institute for Public Policy Research, 1975), pp. 33–34. In Italy, with more nominally compulsory voting, turnout in national elections is normally about 93 percent.

6. Douglas W. Rae, *The Political Consequences of Electoral Laws* (New Haven: Yale University Press, 1971).

7. Two Canadian examples illustrate this point. In the 1935 election in Prince Edward Island, the Conservative party received 42.03 percent of the vote, yet won no seats at all. At

the other extreme, in the 1921 election in Alberta, the United Farmers of Alberta won 67.85 percent of the seats with only 39.49 percent of the vote. While the Canadian multiparty system makes extreme disparities like these more likely, large divergences between votes and seats may be found in any single member plurality system.

8. Anthony Downs, *An Economic Theory of Democracy* (New York: Harper and Row, 1957), chaps. 3, 8; Raphael Zariski, *Italy: The Politics of Uneven Development* (Hinsdale, Ill.: Dryden Press, 1972), pp. 146–47, 194; Leon D. Epstein, *Political Parties in Western Democracies* (New York: Praeger, 1967), pp. 69–70.

9. As John Stuart Mill put it, "as different opinions predominate in different localities, the opinion which is in a minority in some places has a majority in others" (*Considerations on Representative Government* [Chicago: Henry Regnery, 1962], p. 143; see also, Rae, *Political Consequences of Electoral Laws*, chap. 10; John Wildgen, "Electoral Formulae and the Number of Parties," *Journal of Politics* 34 [August 1972]: 943–51).

10. By "optimal enemy" is meant the party, or parties, against which a candidate should concentrate his campaign, either because of the relatively higher value of votes received at their expense or because of the relative ease of attracting votes from them.

11. In principle, all parties will have at least two optimal enemies in each district in PR systems. In fact, if the distribution of parties approaches unidimensionality, or if the distance is great between a party on the outer fringes of the distribution and all other parties, there may be no voters in the region where the "territories" of some pairs of parties abut.

12. Again, this may not be the case for extreme parties if there are no voters whose first preferences lie in the contested region.

13. In fact, if voters are relatively densely located in the center of the political space, and if the number of parties is greater than 2^n, where n is the number of dimensions in the space, then at least one party must find itself completely surrounded by other parties, while those on the extremes will have a positive incentive to converge toward the center. In one dimension, this is the well-known likelihood that center parties will be squeezed out, as happened to the British Liberal party. For two dimensions, the critical number of parties is five. Not coincidentally, this is the number of parties Sartori suggests is one of the conditions leading to "polarized pluralism," in which extreme parties gradually sap the strength of the center. Giovanni Sartori, "European Political Parties: The Case of Polarized Pluralism," in Joseph LaPalombara and Myron Weiner, eds., *Political Parties and Political Development* (Princeton: Princeton University Press, 1966), pp. 137–76; idem, *Parties and Party Systems: A Framework for Analysis* (Cambridge: Cambridge University Press, 1976), pp. 131–72.

14. See Maurice Duverger, *Political Parties* (New York: John Wiley and Sons, 1954).

15. See Joseph LaPalombara, "Decline of Ideology: A Dissent and an Interpretation," *American Political Science Review* 60 (March 1966): 5–16. One should note especially that a center ideology is equally as possible as those of extremists.

16. Duverger, *Political Parties*, pp. 223–26; David Butler and Donald E. Stokes, *Political Change in Britain* (New York: St. Martin's Press, 1969), pp. 326–28. For an alternative view, and responses to it, see John A. Ferejohn and Morris P. Fiorina, "The Paradox of Not Voting: A Decision Theoretic Analysis," *American Political Science Review* 68 (June 1974): 525–35, and the responses by Strom, Stephens, Mayer and Good, Beck, Tullock, Goodin and Roberts, and further remarks by Ferejohn and Fiorina, *American Political Science Review* 69 (September 1975): 908–28.

17. By "local candidates" are meant those for whom the principal "issue" is their ties to the district from which they seek to be elected. Such ties are encouraged under plurality schemes both by the emphasis these formulae place on candidates rather than parties and by the lower thresholds of representation under plurality formulae. Rae, *Political Consequences of Electoral Laws*, chap. 10.

18. Harold Hotelling, "Stability in Competition," *Economic Journal* 39 (March 1929): 47–75. See also, John Clayton Thomas, "The Decline of Ideology in Western Political

Parties: A Study of Changing Policy Orientations," *Sage Contemporary Political Sociology Series*, 1975.

19. This result is suggested jointly by balance theory in psychology and by the work of Arthur Smithies in "Optimal Location in Spatial Competition," *Journal of Political Economy* 49 (June 1941): 423–29.

20. Rusk makes the argument that ballot form influences electoral response by suggesting to people how they "should" think about politics. Jerrold G. Rusk, "The American Electoral Universe: Speculation and Evidence," *American Political Science Review* 68 (September 1974): 1028–49.

21. The campaign of Richard Nixon in 1972 is an example of this. See also, David Leuthold, *Electioneering in a Democracy* (New York: John Wiley and Sons, 1968), esp. p. 116.

22. The Italian *legge truffa* (swindle law), in force for the 1953 election, is an example of such a bonus. It would have given an alliance with 50 percent of the votes plus one two-thirds of the seats in the Chamber of Deputies.

23. Obviously, other measures of district size also might have been considered. For example, square miles of land area or average travel time from one end of the district to the other also might have an impact on campaign behavior.

24. See Henry Valen and David Katz, *Political Parties in Norway* (Oslo: Universitetsforlaget, 1964).

25. David Mayhew discusses credit claiming as a strategy at some length in *Congress: The Electoral Connection* (New Haven: Yale University Press, 1974). He suggests that the structure of the American Congress, especially the prominence of committees and subcommittees and their chairmen, allows members reasonably to claim individual credit both for legislation and for pork barrel benefits for their districts.

26. For example, in the Japanese case a very popular candidate may increase the party's vote while actually reducing the number of seats it wins, and thus hurting his running mates. See Gerald Curtis, *Election Campaigning Japanese Style* (New York: Columbia University Press, 1971), esp. pp. 19–33.

27. Although mentioned by Downs, the problem of resources has received relatively little attention in the rationalistic literature. See, however, Mayhew, *Congress: The Electoral Connection*, pp. 36–44. "What a congressman has to try to do is to insure that in primary and general elections the resource balance . . . favors himself rather than anybody else" (p. 43).

Chapter 3

1. Full sampling and coding information is available in Kenneth Janda, *Political Parties: A Cross National Survey* (New York: Free Press, 1980).

2. When a major institutional or political change in a country came near to the 1956–57 dividing point, as in France with the rise of the Fifth Republic, this was taken as the dividing point between the two subperiods.

3. Kenneth Janda, "A Conceptual Framework for the Comparative Analysis of Political Parties," *Sage Professional Papers in Comparative Politics*, ser. 01-002 (1970).

4. "'Face validity' consists of little more than the subjective determination by the researcher that the indicator actually measures what it purports to measure. . . . 'Content validity' involves the determination that the content of the measure is an adequate and representative sample of the content universe of the property being measured. . . . 'Predictive validity' involves the determination that one indicator can be used to predict accurately a particular value, criterion, or position on some other indicator. . . . 'Construct validity' involves the determination that the indicator relates to other indicators consistent with

theoretically derived hypotheses concerning the concepts (constructs) that are being measured" (Dickinson McGaw and George Watson, *Political and Social Inquiry* [New York: John Wiley and Sons, 1976], pp. 212–13).

5. The correlation (r) with the U.S. experts' ratings is 0.80, and with the Soviet experts' it is 0.76. See Kenneth Janda, "Validating a Conceptual Framework for Comparing Political Parties," *ICPP Reports* no. 18 (March 1978).

6. Hans Daalder and Jerrold G. Rusk, "Perceptions of Party in the Dutch Parliament," in Samuel C. Patterson and John C. Walhke, eds., *Comparative Legislative Behavior* (New York: John Wiley and Sons, 1972), p. 146.

7. M. W. Pedersen, "Preferential Voting in Denmark," *Scandinavian Political Studies* 1 (1966): 167–87.

8. Peter Campbell, *French Electoral Systems* (London: Faber and Faber, 1965).

9. This is not to suggest that parties and politicians in plurality systems are not influenced by ideological considerations. The expectation is, however, that ideology more often will become of conscious and overt importance in PR systems.

10. See C. Waxman, ed., *The Decline of Ideology Debate* (New York: Funk & Wagnalls, 1968); John Clayton Thomas, "The Decline of Ideology in Western Political Parties: A Study of Changing Policy Orientation," *Sage Professional Papers in Contemporary Political Sociology*, ser. 06-012 (1975).

11. See Philip E. Converse, "The Nature of Belief Systems in Mass Publics," in David E. Apter, ed., *Ideology and Discontent* (New York: Free Press, 1964), pp. 206–62; David Butler and Donald E. Stokes, *Political Change in Britain* (London: Macmillan, 1974), pp. 314–37.

12. Rose and Urwin's adoption of Blondel's measure of time in office as an indicator of ideology ignores this fact. Richard Rose and Derek Urwin, "Social Cohesion, Political Parties and Strains in Regimes," *Comparative Political Studies* 2 (April 1969): 7–67; Jean Blondel, "Party Systems and Patterns of Government in Western Democracies," *Canadian Journal of Political Science* 1 (1968): 180–203.

13. Tau-b will achieve its maximum value of 1.0 only if there is a strongly monotonic relationship between the two variables, i.e., if all cases fall on the diagonal. The logical possibility of this occurring is constrained, however, by the marginal distributions of the two variables, so that a value of 1.0 may be impossible in some cases. Gamma will achieve a value of 1.0 for a weakly monotonic relationship. (In the two-by-two case, this means gamma will be 1.0 if one of the four cells is empty.) See Herbert F. Weisberg, "Models of Statistical Relationship," *American Political Science Review* 68 (December 1974): 1638–65.

14. See William Ascher and Sidney Tarrow, "The Stability of Communist Electorates: Evidence from a Longitudinal Analysis of French and Italian Aggregate Data," *American Journal of Political Science* 19 (August 1975): 478–80. Otto Kirschiemer, "The Transformation of the Western European Party Systems," in Joseph LaPalombara and Myron Weiner, eds., *Political Parties and Political Development* (Princeton: Princeton University Press, 1968), pp. 177–200.

15. Converse, "The Nature of Belief Systems in Mass Publics," pp. 206–62. This assumes that voters naturally have low levels of ideological constraint.

16. This might lead one to expect that ideological parties would impose more stringent membership requirements and demand more intensive participation from their members while nonideological parties would be more willing to admit anyone wanting to join regardless of level of commitment. Correlations in the ICPP data suggest that this is indeed the case, especially with regard to participation.

17. See Robert A. Dahl and Edward R. Tufte, *Size and Democracy* (Stanford: Stanford University Press, 1973), for a suggestion that in this kind of argument "small" must be very small indeed.

18. David Mayhew, *Congress: The Electoral Connection* (New Haven: Yale University Press, 1974); Morris Fiorina, "The Case of the Vanishing Marginals: The Bureaucracy Did It," *American Political Science Review* 71 (March 1977): 177–81, implicitly argue against this point, suggesting that patronage and personalism can be of great importance even in the very populous districts of American congressmen.

19. That is, the relationship between district magnitude and issue orientation is weakened but still in the expected direction within each category of electoral choice.

20. Since the ICPP variables in this "cluster" are concerned with the coalescence of two sides of a presumed single split, rather than with the number of factions or simple extent of party disunity, a more general indicator of factionalism cannot be constructed from these variables.

21. On the tendency toward leadership concentration, see Maurice Duverger, *Political Parties* (New York: John Wiley and Sons, 1959), pp. 151–82.

22. For example, see Jeffrey Obler, "The Role of National Party Leaders in the Selection of Parliamentary Candidates: The Belgian Case," *Comparative Politics* 5 (January 1973): 157–84.

23. In the German case, one even could argue that the electoral formula varies within the system, with half the Bundestag elected by a plurality system and the other half by PR.

Chapter 4

1. While true at the time to which this research applies, the British electoral law was amended before the 1974 elections so that party labels now are listed on the ballot.

2. Indeed, candidates have been elected with fewer than 35 percent of the votes and by margins smaller than ten votes. See Peter Richards, *Honourable Members* (London: Faber and Faber, 1959), chap. 1.

3. For a complete description of British electoral law see R. L. Leonard, *Elections in Britain* (London: D. Van Nostrand, 1968); David E. Butler, *The Electoral System in Britain Since 1918* (Oxford: Oxford University Press, 1963).

4. In fact the opinions and prejudices of local elites are tremendously important in determining campaign tactics. See Robert T. Holt and John E. Turner, *Political Parties in Action: The Battle of Barons Court* (New York: Free Press, 1968), chap. 3. Indeed, many MPs simply do what local people tell them to do in campaigning. See chapter 5, below. Likewise, the control of local elites over nominations may be nearly absolute. But these elites, in exercising this control, tend to serve as "nationally oriented cheerleaders" for the national party leadership. Austin Ranney, *Pathways to Parliament* (Madison: University of Wisconsin Press, 1965); idem, "Candidate Selection and Party Cohesion in Britain and the United States," in William J. Crotty, ed., *Approaches to the Study of Party Organization* (Boston: Little, Brown, 1968), pp. 139–58; Leon D. Epstein, "British MPs and Their Local Parties: The Suez Case," *American Political Science Review* 54 (June 1960): 374–90. More recently, the sacking of Dick Taverne, Labour MP for Lincoln, by his constituency party illustrates this point. Even when local elites have been in conflict with their national leaders to the disadvantage of an incumbent MP, the conflicts have tended to be over national policy.

5. The surplus is the difference between the number of first preference votes actually received and the Droop quota. If more than one candidate has more than the quota, the largest surplus is distributed first. Any ballots with no second preference expressed, or with more than one second preference expressed become "nontransferable" and are eliminated from subsequent counts.

6. See Wolfgang Birke, *European Elections by Direct Suffrage* (Leyden: A. W. Sythoff, 1961), chap. 9; Basil Chubb, *The Government and Politics of Ireland* (Stanford: Stanford

University Press, 1970), appendix E; J.F.S. Ross, *The Irish Electoral System* (London: Pall Mall Press, 1959).

7. The party is given some additional control over the allocation of its share of the seats by the fact that a candidate may appear on its list in more than one district or stand for election to the Senate and Chamber of Deputies simultaneously. Since vacancies that occur are filled by the next person on the party's list in the district in which the vacancy occurs, rather than by bye-election, a candidate elected to more than one seat may choose which of two or more candidates will be elected by deciding which seat to accept and which to decline.

8. For example, if no restraints are placed on the shape of the electoral districts, any country could be gerrymandered so that a party with 51 percent of the vote would win every seat, or only 26 percent of the seats, under single-member plurality election with equal population districts. See also, John Loosemore and Victor Hanby, "The Theoretical Limits of Maximum Distortion: Some Analytic Expressions for Electoral Systems," *British Journal of Political Science* 1 (October 1971): 467–78.

9. The best example of this is the shift in 1921 from "first past the post" to PR for elections to the lower house of the Danish parliament at a time when there were four parties. Two-stage plurality schemes in France (twelve parties), the Netherlands (ten parties), Norway (three parties), and Belgium (three parties) also were replaced by PR after the establishment of multiparty competition. See Enid Lakeman and James Lambert, *Voting in Democracies* (London: Faber and Faber, 1955), pp. 150, 159–64, 172–74; and John Grumm, "Theories of Electoral Systems," *Midwest Journal of Political Science* 2 (November 1958): 357–76.

10. Nathaniel Thayer, *How the Conservatives Rule Japan* (Princeton: Princeton University Press, 1969), chap. 5.

11. For example, the one candidate of the Christian Democratic party in Ireland, was denied official recognition. He changed his name by deed-poll to Sean Christian Democrat Loftus in order to get his party's label on the ballot.

12. For example, for inclusion in the ICPP project a party was required to win at least 5 percent of the seats in the national parliament in two successive elections. Richard Rose and Derek Urwin considered all parties for which information was available, with the unfortunate result of systematically undercounting regional parties like the Welsh and Scottish nationalists and the PPST and UV in Italy. Richard Rose and Derek Urwin, "Social Cohesion, Political Parties and Strains in Regimes," *Comparative Political Studies* 2 (April 1969): 6–67.

13. Indeed, in Ireland 10 percent of the deputies elected in 1951 were independents. There has been at least one independent elected in every general election in Ireland, and in most general elections in Britain.

14. See A. John Berrigan, "Interparty Electoral Competition, Stability, and Change: Two-Dimensional and Three-Dimensional Indices," *Comparative Political Studies* 5 (July 1972): 193–210; Edward Cox, "Measurement of Party Strength," *Western Political Quarterly* 13 (December 1960): 1022–42; Paul T. David, "How Can an Index of Party Competition Best Be Derived," *Journal of Politics* 34 (May 1972): 632–38; Douglas W. Rae, "The Concept of Decisiveness in Electoral Outcomes," in Bernhardt Lieberman, ed., *Social Choice* (New York: Gordon and Breach, 1971), pp. 379–92.

15. Douglas W. Rae, *The Political Consequences of Electoral Laws* (New Haven: Yale University Press, 1971), pp. 74–75.

16. Rae defines proportionality as the mean difference between parties' shares of the votes and their shares of the seats (Rae, *Political Consequences of Electoral Laws*, pp. 84, 96–97). This has the problem of giving too much weight to small parties; at the extreme, if the infinite number of (hypothetical) parties that receive no votes and obtain no seats is included, every electoral system would appear perfectly proportional. Rae tries to avoid this by eliminating parties that receive fewer than 2 percent of the vote. This seems unreasonable here, however, since at least in the Italian case it forces the elimination of parties than won significant numbers of seats. Here, proportionality will be measured as the mean absolute deviation between the share of the seats awarded to a party and its share of the votes, computed over all parties that

won at least one seat. By this definition, 0 is the measure of perfect proportionality obtained when vote shares exactly equal seat shares for all parties, while 100 would be perfect disproportionality, obtained only when all the seats are given to parties with no votes.

17. The 1963–68 and 1968–72 figures for the PSI are for the PSI plus PSDI (1963 and 1972) compared to the PSU (1968).

18. Indeed, as Doron and Kronick have shown, the Irish system is potentially perverse in the ultimate sense that "a candidate could win an election if 10,000 people voted for him or her, but would lose that election if he or she received and additional 5,000 votes" (Gideon Doron and Richard Kronick, "Single Transferable Vote: An Example of a Perverse Social Choice Function," *American Journal of Political Science* 21 [May 1977]: 303–11).

19. A party's vote is defined to be "nationalized" to the extent that its local percentages of the vote conform to the model:

$$x_{ik} = n_i + p_i(a_k) + c_{ik}$$

where x_{ik} is its percentage of the total vote in area i at election k; n_i is its normal percentage of the vote in area i; a_k is the national force at election k; c_{ik} is the area specific force at election k; and p_i is a constant (over time), specific to area i. See Richard S. Katz, "The Attribution of Variance in Electoral Returns: An Alternative Measurement Technique," *American Political Science Review* 67 (September 1973): 817–28.

20. For four Irish constituencies it was possible to extend the analysis through the 1965 election. No significant or consistent differences were observed with this six-election series.

21. Chubb, *Government and Politics of Ireland*, chap. 6; Giovanni di Capua, "La scelta dei candidati," in Mattei Dogan and Orazio Petracca, eds., *Partiti politici e strutture sociali in Italia* (Milan: Edizioni di Communita, 1968), pp. 579–608; Leonard, *Elections in Britain*, chap. 6. The Italian Communists, however, have adopted a rather different attitude toward this problem. Tending to value the office of deputy less highly than the other parties, the PCI regularly renews roughly one-third of its parliamentary delegation at each election by replacing incumbents with new candidates on its lists. As the accepted practice, this is generally accepted within the party. When the DC tried to adopt a similar strategy in 1976, primarily by dropping older candidates, it resulted in considerable discomforture within the party. See Gianfranco Pasquino, "Before and After the Italian National Election of 1976," *Government and Opposition* 12 (Winter 1977): 60–87; Douglas Wertman, "The Italian Electoral Process: The Elections of June 1976," in Howard R. Penniman, ed., *Italy at the Polls* (Washington: American Enterprise Institute for Public Policy Research, 1977), pp. 41–80.

22. Actually, the preference vote plays a role even in the partisan defeats, since it determines which incumbents are defeated.

23. This has not always been the case. In early elections, parties often nominated fewer candidates than the total to be elected. In 1948, for example, the DC elected all fourteen of its candidates in Bergamo-Brescia.

24. The impression should not be left that the *capolista* does in fact always head the poll. For example, Alberto Spigaroli, a three-time senator denied renomination in the DC's effort to increase its parliamentary turnover, was made *capolista* in the Parma, Modena, Piacenza, Reggio Emilia constituency but was last among the victorious DC candidates, and that only on a recount.

25. The same general results for the 1976 election may be found in Richard S. Katz and Luciano Bardi, "Voto di preferenza e ricambio del personale parlamentare," *Rivista Italiana di Scienza Politica* 9 (January 1979): 71–95. Similar data for earlier elections may be found in Giovanni Schepis, "Analisi statistica dei resultati," in Alberto Spreafico and Joseph LaPalombara, eds., *Elezioni e comportamento politico in Italia* (Milan: Edizioni di Communita, 1963) p. 384.

26. The number of constituencies is less than thirty-one because there was no identifiable middle part on four DC lists.

27. Luigi D'Amato, *Il voto di preferenza in Italia* (Milan: Giuffre, 1964).

28. More than 65 percent of the votes may cast at least one preference vote, as is illustrated by the fact that Emilio Columbo received preference votes from over 73 percent of the DC voters in his constituency in 1972, even though only 42 percent of the possible preference votes were cast.

29. David Butler and Donald E. Stokes, *Political Change in Britain* (New York: St. Martin's Press, 1969), chap. 10; E. Katz and Paul F. Lazarsfeld, *Personal Influence* (Glencoe, Ill.: Free Press, 1955).

30. Chubb, *Government and Politics of Ireland,* p. 161.

31. Ballots scrutinized on subsequent counts present the problem that those that are nontransferable because they lack third preferences are indistinguishable from those that lack second preferences.

32. This contrasts with the Italian experience with alliances (the PCI-PSI united front in 1948 and the PSU in 1968); in both of these cases the allying parties lost votes from the preceding election and gained in the election following the breakup of the alliance. See also, Peter Campbell, *French Electoral Systems* (London: Faber and Faber, 1965), p. 117 for the French experience.

33. Paul M. Sacks, "Bailiwicks, Locality, and Religion: Three Elements in an Irish Dail Constituency Elections," *Economic and Social Review* 1 (July 1970): 531–54.

34. See also, Mart Bax, "Patronage Irish Style: Irish Politicians as Brokers," *Sociologische Gids* 17 (May–June 1970): 179–91.

Chapter 5

1. See, for example, David Butler and Donald E. Stokes, *Political Change in Britain* (New York: St. Martin's Press, 1969); Donald E. Stokes, "Parties and the Nationalization of Electoral Forces," in W. N. Chambers and W. D. Burnham, eds., *The American Party Systems: Stages of Political Development* (New York: Oxford University Press, 1967), pp. 182–202.

2. Richard S. Katz, "The Attribution of Variance in Electoral Returns: An Alternative Measurement Technique," *American Political Science Review* 67 (September 1973): 817–28.

3. All relationships referred to in this chapter are significant at the level of $p < 0.05$ or better unless otherwise stated.

4. See Giorgio Galli and Alfonso Prandi, *Patterns of Political Participation in Italy* (New Haven: Yale University Press, 1970), pp. 49–55.

5. Jay G. Blumler, "Mass Media Roles and Reaction in the February Election," in Howard R. Penniman, ed., *Britain at the Polls* (Washington: American Enterprise Institute for Public Policy Research, 1974), pp. 131–62; William E. Porter, "The Mass Media in the Italian Elections of 1976," in Howard R. Penniman, ed., *Italy at the Polls* (Washington: American Enterprise Institute for Public Policy Research, 1977), pp. 259–86.

6. Katz, "Attribution of Variance in Electoral Returns," p. 824.

7. Paul M. Sacks, "Bailiwicks, Locality, and Religion: Three Elements in an Irish Dail Constituency Election," *Economic and Social Review* 1 (July 1970): 531–54.

8. Basil Chubb, *The Government and Politics of Ireland* (Stanford: Stanford University Press, 1970), pp. 153–56.

9. *Dundalk Democrat*, 2 March 1957.

10. Respondents were asked to check the range in which their parties' expenses fell. In computing the averages cited, the top of the range always was used.

11. R. L. Leonard, *Elections in Britain* (London: D. Van Nostrand, 1968), pp. 151–55.

12. *Informa tutto* (Selezione della Reader's Digest, 1973).

13. See Leonard, *Elections in Britain,* chap. 3. Also, compare the accounts of the national campaigns in David Butler, *The British General Election of 1955* (London: Frank Cass, 1955) and David Butler and Anthony King, *The British General Election of 1966* (New York: St. Martin's Press, 1966).

14. See Leonard, *Elections in Britain,* chap. 8; Robert Holt and John Turner, *Political Parties in Action: The Battle of Barons Court* (New York: Free Press, 1968), chap. 3.

15. Joseph LaPalombara, *Interest Groups in Italian Politics* (Princeton: Princeton University Press, 1964), pp. 207–12; idem, *The Italian Labor Movement: Problems and Prospects* (Ithaca, N.Y.: Cornell University Press, 1957), pp. 78–96; Galli and Prandi, *Patterns of Political Participation in Italy,* chap. 5.

16. Austin Ranney, *Pathways to Parliament* (Madison: University of Wisconsin Press, 1965); Leon D. Epstein, "British MPs and their Local Parties: The Suez Case," *American Political Science Review* 54 (June 1960): 374–90. See also, Richard Rose, "The Political Ideas of English Party Activists," *American Political Science Review* 56 (June 1962): 360–71; Roland Young, *The British Parliament* (Evanston, Ill.: Northwestern University Press, 1962), pp. 230–31; Robert Jackson, *Rebels and Whips* (New York: St. Martin's Press, 1968), chap. 10.

17. Peter Richards, *Honourable Members* (London: Faber and Faber, 1959), chap. 1; Leonard, *Elections in Britain,* pp. 67–74; Frank Stacey, *The Government of Modern Britain* (Oxford: Oxford University Press, 1968), chap. 3.

18. Chubb, *Government and Politics of Ireland,* pp. 150–53; Paul M. Sacks, *The Donegal Mafia* (New Haven: Yale University Press, 1976), chap. 5.

19. Giovanni DiCapua, "La scelta dei candidati," in Mattei Dogan and Orazio Maria Petracca, eds., *Partiti politici e strutture sociali in Italia* (Milan: Edizioni di Communita, 1968), pp. 579–608.

20. Richards, *Honourable Members,* p. 27.

21. While this statement clearly was true until the late 1960s, in recent years the personal views of candidates have come to play a greater role, especially in the Labour party. The sacking of Reg Prentice by his constituency party, apparently for supporting Harold Wilson's policies *too* loyally, illustrates this new trend.

22. Mart Bax, "Patronage Irish Style: Irish Politicians as Brokers," *Sociologische Gids* 17 (May–June 1970): 179–91.

23. Patrick Seyd, "Factionalism Within the Conservative Party: The Monday Club," *Government and Opposition* 7 (Autumn 1972): 464–87.

Chapter 6

1. As mentioned above, this was changed before the 1974 general election.

2. Henry Pelling, *The Origins of the Labour Party* (Oxford: Clarendon Press, 1965); R. T. McKenzie, *British Political Parties* (London: Allen and Unwin, 1958).

3. Richard Rose, *Politics in England* (Boston: Little, Brown, 1974), p. 288.

4. Robert D. Putnam, *The Beliefs of Politicians* (New Haven: Yale University Press, 1973), chap. 6.

5. John Lees and Richard Kimber, eds., *Political Parties in Modern Britain* (London: Routledge and Kegan Paul, 1972), pp. 14–16.

6. Rose, *Politics in England,* pp. 301–2.

7. David Butler, "American Myths About British Parties," *Virginia Quarterly Review* 31 (Winter 1955): 47–52.

8. Rose, *Politics in England*, p. 304.

9. David Butler, "The Paradox of Party Difference," *American Behavioral Scientist* 4 (1960): 3–5.

10. See David Robertson, app. IV, in David Butler and Michael Pinto-Duschinsky, *The British General Election of 1970* (New York: St. Martin's Press, 1971).

11. Rose, *Politics in England*, p. 308.

12. T. Brennan, *Politics and Government in Britain* (Cambridge: Cambridge University Press, 1972), p. 144.

13. Rose, *Politics in England*, pp. 312–14.

14. Robert Jackson, *Rebels and Whips* (New York: St. Martin's Press, 1968), pp. 4–5.

15. For a reasonably complete list of such groups, see Harry Mitchell and Phyllis Birt, *Who Does What in Parliament* (London: Mitchell and Birt, 1972).

16. For example, see Richard Rose, "The Bow Group's Role in British Politics," *Western Political Quarterly* 14 (December 1961): 865–78; Patrick Seyd, "Factionalism Within the Conservative Party: The Monday Club," *Government and Opposition* 7 (Autumn 1972): 464–87; Herbert Lord Morrison of Lambeth, *Government and Parliament* (Oxford: Oxford University Press, 1964), pp. 137–39, 144–46.

17. John P. MacKintosh, "Reform of the House of Commons: The Case for Specialization," in Gerhard Loewenberg, ed., *Modern Parliaments: Change or Decline?* (Chicago: Atherton, 1971), pp. 40–49.

18. Samuel Finer et al., *Backbench Opinion in the House of Commons* (New York: Pergamon Books, 1961).

19. Lord Morrison of Lambeth, *Government and Parliament*, pp. 141–44; Jackson, *Rebels and Whips*, chap. 11.

20. Brennan, *Politics and Government in Britain*, pp. 142–44.

21. Maurice Manning, *Irish Political Parties* (Dublin: Gill and Macmillan, 1972), pp. 9–62.

22. Basil Chubb, *The Government and Politics of Ireland* (Stanford: Stanford University Press, 1970), p. 159.

23. Examples for 1973 include Deputies Dockrell, Costello, O'Higgins, and Crowley. See also, Chubb, *Government and Politics of Ireland*, pp. 151–53.

24. See Brian Farrell, *Chairman or Chief? The Role of Taoiseach in Irish Government* (Dublin: Gill and Macmillan, 1971), pp. 79–81; Paul M. Sacks, *The Donegal Mafia* (New Haven: Yale University Press, 1976), chap. 10.

25. Chubb, *Government and Politics of Ireland*, pp. 153–54.

26. Ibid.

27. See Morley Ayearst, *The Republic of Ireland: Its Government and Politics* (New York: New York University Press, 1970); Chubb, *Government and Politics of Ireland*, chap. 8.

28. Chubb, *Government and Politics of Ireland*, pp. 183–84.

29. Ibid., pp. 168–76.

30. Mart Bax, "Patronage Irish Style: Irish Politicians as Brokers," *Sociologische Gids* 17 (May–June 1970): 179–91.

31. Chubb, *Government and Politics of Ireland*, pp. 196–97.

32. Stefano Passigli, "Comparative Party Finance: Italy," *Journal of Politics* 25 (November 1963): 726.

33. Raphael Zariski, *Italy: The Politics of Uneven Development* (Hinsdale, Ill.: Dryden Press, 1972), p. 148.

34. See Norman Kogan, *A Political History of Postwar Italy* (London: Pall Mall Press, 1966), chap. 12; Zariski, *Italy*, pp. 170–71.

35. Giorgio Galli and Alfonso Prandi, *Patterns of Political Participation in Italy* (New Haven: Yale University Press, 1970), pp. 255–301.

36. Putnam, *Beliefs of Politicians*, chap. 6.

37. Galli and Prandi, *Patterns of Political Participation in Italy*, chap. 5.

38. Michele Sernini, *Le correnti nel partito* (Milan: Istituto Editoriale Cisalpino, 1966), chap. 1.

39. Zariski, *Italy*, pp. 162–65.

40. Alberto Spreafico and Franco Cazzola, "Correnti di partito e processi di identificazione," *Il Politico* 35 (1970): 198.

41. Dante Germino and Stefano Passigli, *The Government and Politics of Contemporary Italy* (New York: Harper and Row, 1968), p. 129; Zariski, *Italy*, p. 149.

42. Spreafico and Cazzola, "Correnti di partito," pp. 199–200.

43. Ibid., p. 206.

44. Zariski, *Italy*, pp. 168–74; Galli and Prandi, *Patterns of Political Participation in Italy*, pp. 18–19.

45. See Giovanni Sartori, "Proporzionalismo, frazionismo e crisi dei partiti," *Rivista Italiana di Scienza Politica* 1 (December 1971): 629–55. A complete list of the factional identifications of DC deputies and senators appeared in *Paese Sera,* 16 May 1972.

46. Zariski, *Italy*, pp. 149, 171.

47. For a particularly critical view of the DC as a party interested only in retaining power, see Michele Sernini, *La disputa sui partito* (Padua: Marsilio Editori, 1968), esp. p. 141.

48. Gianfranco Pasquino, "Le radici dei frazionismo e il voto di preferenza," *Rivista Italiana di Scienza Politica* 2 (August 1972): 364.

49. Robert Gilsdorf, "Factionalism in the Italian Christian Democratic Party, 1958, 1963," (Ph.D. diss., Yale University, 1970), chap. 5.

50. Zariski, *Italy*, p. 148.

51. Reported in *Unita*, 22 April 1964.

Chapter 7

1. Maurice Duverger, *Political Parties*, trans. Barbara and Robert North, (New York: John Wiley and Sons, 1959), p. 217.

2. See Robert D. Putnam, *The Comparative Study of Political Elites* (Englewood Cliffs, N.J.: Prentice-Hall, 1976), chap. 2.

3. James David Barber, *The Lawmakers* (New Haven: Yale University Press, 1965); idem, *The Presidential Character* (Englewood Cliffs, N.J.: Prentice-Hall, 1972); Putnam, *Comparative Study of Political Elites*, chap. 4.

4. Brian Barry, *Sociologists, Economists, and Democracy* (London: Collier-Macmillan, 1970), pp. 14–23; William H. Riker and Peter C. Ordeshook, "A Theory of the Calculus of Voting," *American Political Science Review* 62 (March 1968): 25–43; John A. Ferejohn and Morris P. Fiorina, "The Paradox of Not Voting: A Decision Theoretic Analysis," *American Political Science Review* 68 (June 1974): 525–35.

5. "Citizen duty" as introduced by Riker and Ordeshook has the ring of such a *post hoc* explanation. To say that people vote because they feel they should begs the real question of why they feel that way.

6. Economists, in contrast, have found a reasonable assumption—that everyone is motivated by a desire for wealth—that allows them to theorize about mass economic behavior. In this context, the fact that the assumption is over simple often makes no substantial difference.

7. Robert Michels, *Political Parties*, trans. Eden and Cedar Paul (New York: Free Press, 1962) is one of the forerunners of this concern. See also, Austin Ranney, *The Doctrine of Responsible Party Government* (Urbana: University of Illinois Press, 1962).

8. Frank Goodnow, *Politics and Administration* (New York: Macmillan, 1900), pp. 27–28.

9. Ibid., p. 234.

10. John Stuart Mill, *Considerations on Representative Government* (Chicago: Henry Regnery, 1962), chap. 3.

11. E. E. Schattschneider, *Party Government* (New York: Rinehart and Winston, 1942), pp. 57–59.

12. Hanna F. Pitkin, *The Concept of Representation* (Berkeley: University of California Press, 1967); J. Roland Pennock and John W. Chapman, eds., *Representation* (New York: Atherton, 1968).

13. See Robert Weissberg, "Collective vs. Dyadic Representation in Congress," *American Political Science Review* 72 (June 1978): 535–47; Pitkin, *Concept of Representation*, chap. 8; Alfred DeGrazia, *Public and Republic* (New York: Alfred A. Knopf, 1951), pp. 36–45.

14. M. G. Kendall and A. Stuart, "The Law of Cubic Proportion in Election Returns," *British Journal of Sociology* 1 (September 1950): 183–96; Terence H. Qualter, "An Application of the Cube Law to the Canadian Electoral System," *Canadian Journal of Political Science* 1 (September 1968): 336–44; Edward R. Tufte, "The Relationship Between Seats and Votes in Two-Party Systems," *American Political Science Review* 67 (June 1973): 540–54.

15. A. J. Milnor, *Elections and Political Stability* (Boston: Little, Brown, 1969), p. 37.

16. Arend Lijphart, *The Politics of Accommodation* (Berkeley: University of California Press, 1975).

17. Duverger, *Political Parties*, p. 7.

18. See Samuel H. Beer, *British Politics in the Collectivist Age* (New York: Vintage Books, 1969), chap. 3.

19. Milnor, *Elections and Political Stability*, pp. 30–39.

20. In fact, many real systems of ordinal choice may produce less accurate representation. Where panachage allows voters to pick a number of candidates regardless of party in a system otherwise oriented toward lists, a vote for an individual candidate is counted as a partial vote for his list as well as counting as a preference vote for him. Thus, if the candidate receiving the split vote is ranked highly, or lowly, enough without the split votes he receives so that they make no difference to his personal chances of election, the effect of those votes will be to further the election of *other* candidates of his party.

21. Similar problems arise with bureaucratic reforms that ignore the private interests—such as security of tenure and advancement—of officials. See Joseph LaPalombara, *Politics Within Nations* (Englewood Cliffs, N.J.: Prentice-Hall, 1974), chap. 8.

22. Reforms in the United States imposed by the federal courts are obviously exceptions to this rule.

Index

ACLI. *See* Italian Association of Christian
  Workers
Alliances, interparty, 29, 34
  Eire, 80–81
  Italy, 142
Amendola, Giorgio, 113
Andreotti, Giulio, 112
Australia
  electoral system, 38–39
  voter turnout, 135
Austria
  electoral system, 38–39
Avanti!, 93

Belgium
  electoral formula and number of parties,
    140
Bow Group, 103

Campaign, electoral
  finance, 90–92
    party cohesion and, 9
  organization, 88–93
    district magnitude and, 31, 33
    intraparty choice and, 31–32, 34
  resources, 32, 34, 54, 57, 88–93, 137
  techniques, 87–90
Canada
  election results, 135–36
  electoral system, 38–39
Canvassing
  for election, 30–31, 89
  for nomination, 98
Career advancement, 7–8, 9
Case studies, 10
Categoric choice, 28–29
Catholic Action, 93, 109–10, 112

CGIL, 109, 111
CISL, 109, 111
Citizen duty, 145
Clarity as indicator of issue orientation,
  48–50
Colley, George, 113
Coltivatori diretti, 109, 112
Columbo, Emilio, 142
Communism
  weakness of, in Britain, 2
Competitive constellation, 66, 70
Compromesso storico, 109
Confederation of British Industry, 93
Consistency as indicator of ideology, 46
Cosgrave, Liam, 106
Cosgrave, W. T., 105–6

DeMartino, Francesco, 110
Democracy
  elections and, 1–2
  modern, defined, 1–2
Denmark
  electoral formula and number of
    parties, 140
  electoral system, 38–39
  intraparty choice, 40
deValera, Eamon, 105
Direct primary
  Costa Rica, 134
  United States, 8, 31
Disraeli, Benjamin, 2
District boundaries and plurality
  election, 64, 140
District magnitude, 30, 48
  campaign organization and, 31
  Eire, 62
  Great Britain, 61
  ideology and, 31, 33

District magnitude (cont.)
  issue orientation and, 30, 33, 36,
    48–52, 139
  Italy, 63–64
  localism and, 30, 48
  number of parties, competitive constella-
    tions, and, 31, 33, 67
  party cohesion and, 34
  patronage and, 30, 33
Doctrinism as indicator of ideology, 47
Donat-Cattin, Carlo, 111

Economic approach. *See* Rationalistic
    paradigm
Eire
  Blueshirts, 105
  campaign organization, 89–90, 94, 105
  campaign resources, 85–93
  Center party, 105
  Cumann na nGaedheal, 105–6
  election results, 72–73
  electoral system, 38–39, 40, 61–62
  Fianna Fail, 105–6
    intraparty choice, 82
    leadership selection, 113–14
  Fine Gael, 105–6
    coalition with Labour, 80–81, 106
    factionalism, 56
    ideological style, 44, 45
    issue orientation, 50, 51, 52
    issue positions, 44
  interparty alliances, 80–81
  intraparty choice, 79–83
  intraparty turnover, 71–73
  issues, 86, 106
  nationalization of electoral change, 70–71
  nomination, 79–80, 105
    criteria, 95, 97
    process, 95
  number of parties and competitive
    constellations, 67
  parties
    cohesion, 108
    issue orientation, 5, 107–8
    representation, 108
    social bases of support, 106
  proportionality and interparty turnover,
    68–70
  Sinn Fein, 105
  transfer of votes, 80–81
Elections
  free, 1

Electoral behavior, 18–19
Electoral formula, 20–21, 40
  ideology and, 21–28, 33, 36, 40–48
  interparty turnover and, 68–70
  number of parties, competitive constella-
    tions, and, 47, 65–68
  proportionality and, 20–21, 68–70
  representation and, 120–22
Electoral law. *See* Electoral system
Electoral system
  electoral law, 19–20, 32–33, 64
  district magnitude, 30–31
  electoral formula, 20–21, 40
  intraparty electoral choice, 31–32, 40
  nature of choice, 28–29
  party cohesion and, 8, 9–10
  rational action and, 13, 17–18
  reform, 123
Epstein, Leon, 8
Extremism and ideology, 41–46

Fanfani, Amintore, 112
Federalism and party cohesion, 8
Finance. *See* Campaign, electoral
Forlani, Arnaldo, 112
Forze Libere, 93
France
  Communist party
    cohesion, 56, 58
    ideological style, 43, 44, 45
    issue orientation, 50, 51, 52
    issue positions, 54
  electoral formula and number of
    parties, 140
  electoral system, 38–39
  intraparty electoral choice, 40
Friends of Tribune, 103–4

Germany
  electoral formula, 139
  electoral system, 38–39
  Weimar Republic, 2
Gerrymander, 140
Giolitti, Antonio, 110
Giorno, Il, 93
Great Britain
  ballot, 61, 101, 139
  campaign organization, 89–90, 92
  campaign resources, 85–93
  spending limitation, 90

Conservative party, 101–4
  cohesion, 6, 56, 58, 103–4
  ideological style, 44, 45
  issue orientation, 50, 51, 52
  issue positions, 44, 101–2
election results, 72, 73
electoral system, 20, 38–39, 61
Independent Labour party, 114
issues, 86, 102–3
Labour party, 101–4
  cohesion, 6, 103–4
  nomination, 96–97
nationalization of electoral change,
  70–71, 87
nomination, 7, 94, 100
  criteria, 95, 96–98
  process, 94–95
number of parties and competitive
  constellations, 67
parliament, committees in, 103–4
parties, 61, 100–105
  career advancement, 7
  cohesion, 7–8, 103–4, 114
  committees, 103
  European Economic Community and,
    102–3
  groups within, 103–4
  issue orientation, 5, 7, 101–4
  leadership selection, 9
  representation, 104–5
  social bases of support, 101
party system, 2
proportionality and interparty turnover,
  68–70
reasons for effective government, 2
Groups and the rationalistic paradigm,
  11–12

Haughey, Charles, 113
Heath, Edward, 102

Iceland
  electoral system, 38–39
Ideology
  definition, 24
  district magnitude and, 31, 33
  electoral formula and, 21–28, 33, 36,
    40–48
  indicators of, 41–42, 46–47
Incremental proportionality. *See*
  Proportionality

International Comparative Political Parties
  Project, 16, 36–37, 48–49, 140
Interparty turnover, 68–70
Intrapartisan defeat. *See* Intraparty turnover
Intraparty choice, 31–32, 40
  cohesion and, 31–32, 34, 36, 53–58
  Denmark, 40
  Eire, 62, 79–83
  France, 40
  Italy, 63, 74–79, 142
  Japan, 9–10
  Netherlands, 40
  United States, 8
Intraparty competition for resources,
  91–93
Intraparty turnover, 71–73, 75–76
Ireland. *See* Eire
Israel
  electoral formula, 20–21
Issue
  defined, 18
  importance, 85–87
Issue orientation
  district magnitude and, 30, 33, 36,
    48–52, 139
  indicators of, 48–50
  nature of choice and, 29, 34, 36, 52–53
Italian Association of Christian Workers
  (ACLI), 93, 111, 112
Italy
  campaign organization, 90–91, 108–9
  campaign resources, 85–94
  Christian Democratic party (DC), 93,
    111–13
  Communist party (PCI), 109, 113, 141
  compromesso storico, 109
  economic problems, 2
  election results, 72–73
  electoral system, 38–39, 63–64, 141
  interest groups, 109–10
  interparty alliances, 142
  intraparty choice, 63, 74–79, 142
  intraparty turnover, 71–73, 75–76
  Italian Social Movement (MSI), 110
  nationalization of electoral change, 70–71
  nomination, 74
    criteria, 96, 97, 98–99
    process, 95
  number of parties and competitive
    constellations, 67
  parties
    cohesion, 5, 110–13

Italy (cont.)
  ideological nature, 109
  issue orientation, 5
  representation, 113
  social bases of support, 109–10
  Popular party, 111
  proportionality and intraparty turnover,
    68–70
  Republican party (PRI), 110
  Social-Democratic party (PSDI), 110–12
  Socialist party (PSI), 110–12
    union with Social-Democrats, 110
  Socialist Party of Proletarian Unity
    (PSIUP), 110–11

Japan
  campaign finance, 9
  electoral system, 9–10, 31, 137
  Liberal Democratic party, 8–10, 65

Leadership concentration as indicator
    of party cohesion, 54–55, 57
Leadership selection and party cohesion, 9
LeMass, Sean, 106
Localism, 136
  district magnitude and, 30–31, 33, 48
  nature of choice and, 29
  party cohesion and, 8
Loftus, Sean, 140
Lombardi, Ricardo, 110
Luxembourg
  electoral system, 38–39
Lynch, Jack, 113

Mancini, Giacomo, 110–11
Mass media, 31, 88
Mayhew, David, 137
Members of parliament and rationality, 12
Monday Club, 98, 103, 104
Moro, Aldo, 112

National Farmers' Union, 93
National Hydrocarbons Trust (ENI),
    93, 112
Nationalization of electoral change, 70–71,
    86–87, 115–16, 141
National Peasants' Alliance, 109
Nature of choice, 28–29
  issue orientation and, 29, 52–53

representation and, 122–23
Nenni, Pietro, 110
Netherlands
  electoral formula and number of
    parties, 140
  electoral system, 38–39
  intraparty choice, 40
New Zealand
  electoral system, 38–39
Nomination, 94–99
  Italy, 74
  party cohesion and, 7
Norway
  electoral formula and number of
    parties, 140
Number of parties, 65–67
  electoral formula and, 23, 26, 67–68, 140
  ideology and, 67

O'Duffy, General Gavin, 106
Optimal enemy
  defined, 136
  number of, 23, 26, 136
Ordinal choice, 28–29
Osservatore Romano, 93

Panachage, 146
Parliamentary government and party
    cohesion, 8
Parliamentary parties. See Parties
Parties
  cohesion, 3–4, 6–10
    indicators of, 54–55
    intraparty choice and, 31–32, 34,
      36, 53–58
  defined, 4, 65–67, 140
  democracy and, 1, 119–20
  functions, 4
  internal democracy, 119–20
  issue orientation, 3–5
  membership and ideology, 138
  number, 65–67, 140
  parliamentary, 5, 12
  platform, 18–19, 135
  system, 2–3, 65–68
Partisan defeat. See Intraparty turnover
Patronage, 30, 33, 137, 139
Personalism, 29–30, 33
PEST, 103
Plurality election, 20–21
  ideology and, 24–28, 33, 36, 40–48, 138

interparty turnover and, 68–70
number of parties and competitive
    constellations, 65–68
proportionality, 68–70, 135–36
representation and, 120–22
Polarized pluralism, 2, 136
Policy debate as indicator of issue
    orientation, 49
Politico, 93
Preference vote. *See* Intraparty choice
Prentice, Reg, 134, 143
Proportionality, 68–70, 140–41
Proportional representation, 20–21
ideology and, 21–24, 33, 36, 40–48, 138
interparty turnover and, 68–70
number of parties and competitive
    constellations, 65–68
proportionality, 68–70, 135–36
representation and, 120–22
Purposive incentives as indicator of
    issue orientation, 48, 50

RADAR, 93
Rae, Douglas W., 20, 28, 30, 40–41
Ranney, Austin, 7, 134
Rationalistic paradigm, 10–12, 15, 117–19
Rationality, 12
Representation, 120–22
    Eire, 107
    Great Britain, 105
    Italy, 113
    nature of choice and, 122–23, 146
    party system and, 3–4
Resource mobilization, 32, 137
Responsible two-party government, 2–3
Rippon, Geoffry, 103

Sartori, Giovanni, 141
Select Committee on Agriculture, 104
Select Committee on Science and
        Technology, 104
Self-interest, 11–13

Single nontransferable vote, 9–10, 137
Single transferable vote, 40, 61–62
Spigaroli, Alberto, 141
Sturzo, Luigi, 111
Sweden, electoral system, 38–39

Tanassi, Mario, 110
Taverne, Dick, 4
Thayer, Nathaniel, 9–10
Theory. *See also* Rationalistic paradigm
    paradigm, 11
    simplification, 35
    testing, 14–15, 35–36
Trades Union Congress, 93
Turnout, 19, 135, 145
Turnover
    interparty, 68–70
    intraparty, 71–73, 75–76

UIL, 109, 111
Union of Italian Women, 110
Union of Women, 109–10
Unita, 93
United Kingdom. *See* Great Britain
United States
    campaign finance, 9
    Democratic party
        cohesion, 56, 58
        ideological style, 44, 45
        issue orientation, 50, 51, 52, 55
        issue positions, 44
    electoral system, 20, 38–39
    intraparty choice, 31
    parties
        cohesion, 8
        issue orientation, 6–7
    Republican party, 57

Validity, 37, 137–38

Wilson, Harold, 102, 143

The Johns Hopkins University Press

This book was composed in Quadritek Times Roman text
and display by Brushwood Graphics. It was printed
and bound by Universal Lithographers, Inc.

Date Due